Sungsoo Pyo
Editor

Benchmarks in Hospitality and Tourism

Benchmarks in Hospitality and Tourism has been co-published simultaneously as *Journal of Quality Assurance in Hospitality & Tourism*, Volume 2, Numbers 3/4 2001.

Pre-publication REVIEWS, COMMENTARIES, EVALUATIONS . . .

"Contains a range of PRACTICAL AND WELL-WRITTEN ARTICLES. Consideration of these would benefit practitioners within hospitality and students and academics interested in the related topics of benchmarking, quality management, customer satisfaction, customer retention, etc."

Dr. David Bowen
School of Hotel and Restaurant Management
Oxford Brookes University
United Kingdom

More pre-publication
REVIEWS, COMMENTARIES, EVALUATIONS . . .

"A SUPERB COMPILATION of articles on benchmarking concepts and practices. . . . Will provide insight to anyone involved in hospitality and tourism management. AN INVALUABLE SOURCE FOR GRADUATE AND DOCTORAL RESEARCH AND EDUCATION."

Sitki Gozlu, PhD
Professor
Faculty of Management
Istanbul Technical University
Turkey

"UNIQUE . . . offers an effective overview of the concept, especially as it applies to the hospitality industry. . . . APPROPRIATE AS AN ANCILLARY TEXT FOR CASE STUDIES AND ANALYSES FOR A GRADUATE-LEVEL COURSE that covers the concept of bench marking."

Vivienne Wildes, PhD, Director
Undergraduate Fellowships Office
and Affiliate Assistant Professor
of Hotel, Restaurant
and Institutional Management
The Pennsylvania State University
University Park

"PROVIDES IN-DEPTH KNOWLEDGE, UNDERSTANDING, AND PRACTICAL APPLICATIONS. . . . This book will be of value to academics and students involved in any area of service/quality management."

Ray Pine, PhD
Professor
School of Hotel & Tourism Management
The Hong Kong Polytechnic University

"A HANDY SINGLE VOLUME that clearly explains the principles and current thinking about benchmarking, plus useful insights on how the techniques can be converted into profitable business operations. Includes conceptual, practical, and operational (or 'how-it-is-done') chapters."

Chris Ryan, PhD, MEd, MPhil BSc (Econ) Hons
Professor of Tourism
The University of Waikato
Hamilton, New Zealand

The Haworth Hospitality Press

Benchmarks in Hospitality and Tourism

Benchmarks in Hospitality and Tourism has been co-published simultaneously as *Journal of Quality Assurance in Hospitality & Tourism,* Volume 2, Numbers 3/4 2001.

The *Journal of Quality Assurance in Hospitality & Tourism*™ Monographic "Separates"

Executive Editor: Sungsoo Pyo

Below is a list of "separates," which in serials librarianship means a special issue simultaneously published as a special journal issue or double-issue *and* as a "separate" hardbound monograph. (This is a format which we also call a "DocuSerial.")

"Separates" are published because specialized libraries or professionals may wish to purchase a specific thematic issue by itself in a format which can be separately cataloged and shelved, as opposed to purchasing the journal on an on-going basis. Faculty members may also more easily consider a "separate" for classroom adoption.

"Separates" are carefully classified separately with the major book jobbers so that the journal tie-in can be noted on new book order slips to avoid duplicate purchasing.

You may wish to visit Haworth's website at . . .

http://www.HaworthPress.com

. . . to search our online catalog for complete tables of contents of these separates and related publications.

You may also call 1-800-HAWORTH (outside US/Canada: 607-722-5857), or Fax 1-800-895-0582 (outside US/Canada: 607-771-0012), or e-mail at:

getinfo@haworthpressinc.com

Benchmarks in Hospitality and Tourism, edited by Sungsoo Pyo (Vol. 2, No. 3/4, 2001). *"A HANDY SINGLE VOLUME that clearly explains the principles and current thinking about benchmarking, plus useful insights on how the techniques can be converted into profitable business operations. Includes conceptual, practical, and operational (or 'how-it-is-done') chapters." (Chris Ryan, PhD, MEd, MPhil, BSc (Econ) Hons, Professor of Tourism, The University of Waikato, Hamilton, New Zealand)*

Benchmarks in Hospitality and Tourism

Sungsoo Pyo
Editor

Benchmarks in Hospitality and Tourism has been co-published simultaneously as *Journal of Quality Assurance in Hospitality & Tourism,* Volume 2, Numbers 3/4 2001.

The Haworth Hospitality Press
An Imprint of
The Haworth Press, Inc.
New York • London

Published by

The Haworth Hospitality Press®, 10 Alice Street, Binghamton, NY 13904-1580 USA

The Haworth Hospitality Press® is an imprint of The Haworth Press, Inc., 10 Alice Street, Binghamton, NY 13904-1580 USA.

Benchmarks in Hospitality and Tourism has been co-published simultaneously as *Journal of Quality Assurance in Hospitality & Tourism,* Volume 2, Numbers 3/4 2001.

Cover design by Thomas J. Mayshock Jr.

Library of Congress Cataloging-in-Publication Data

Benchmarks in hospitality and tourism / Sungsoo Pyo, editor.
p. cm.
"Has been co-published simultaneously as Journal of quality assurance in hospitality & tourism, volume 2, numbers 3/4 2001."
Includes bibliographical references and index.
ISBN 0-7890-1914-0 (hard : alk. paper)–ISBN 0-7890-1915-9 (pbk : alk. paper)
1. Benchmarking (Management) 2. Hospitality industry–Management. 3. Tourism–Management. I. Pyo, Sungsoo. II. Journal of quality assurance in hospitality & tourism.

HD62.15 .B462 2002
647.94′068′4–dc21

2002008190

Indexing, Abstracting & Website/Internet Coverage

This section provides you with a list of major indexing & abstracting services. That is to say, each service began covering this periodical during the year noted in the right column. Most Websites which are listed below have indicated that they will either post, disseminate, compile, archive, cite or alert their own Website users with research-based content from this work. (This list is as current as the copyright date of this publication.)

Abstracting, Website/Indexing Coverage . . . . Year When Coverage Began

- ***CIRET (Centre International de Recherches et d' Etudes Touristiques). Computerized Touristique & General Bibliography <www.ciret-tourism.com>*** **2000**
- ***CNPIEC Reference Guide: Chinese National Directory of Foreign Periodicals*** **2000**
- ***FINDEX <www.publist.com>*** **2000**
- ***INSPEC <www.iee.org.uk/publish/>*** **2000**
- ***Leisure, Recreation & Tourism Abstracts (c/o CAB Intl/CAB ACCESS) <www.cabi.org>*** **2000**
- ***Management & Marketing Abstracts*** **2000**
- ***South African Assn for Food Science & Technology (SAAFOST)*** **2000**
- ***TOURISM: an international interdisciplinary journal*** **2000**

(continued)

- ***"Travel Research Bookshelf" a current awareness service of the Journal of Travel Research "Abstracts from other Journals Section" published by the Travel & Tourism Association*** **2000**
- ***World Publishing Monitor*** **2000**

Special Bibliographic Notes related to special journal issues (separates) and indexing/abstracting:

- indexing/abstracting services in this list will also cover material in any "separate" that is co-published simultaneously with Haworth's special thematic journal issue or DocuSerial. Indexing/abstracting usually covers material at the article/chapter level.
- monographic co-editions are intended for either non-subscribers or libraries which intend to purchase a second copy for their circulating collections.
- monographic co-editions are reported to all jobbers/wholesalers/approval plans. The source journal is listed as the "series" to assist the prevention of duplicate purchasing in the same manner utilized for books-in-series.
- to facilitate user/access services all indexing/abstracting services are encouraged to utilize the co-indexing entry note indicated at the bottom of the first page of each article/chapter/contribution.
- this is intended to assist a library user of any reference tool (whether print, electronic, online, or CD-ROM) to locate the monographic version if the library has purchased this version but not a subscription to the source journal.
- individual articles/chapters in any Haworth publication are also available through the Haworth Document Delivery Service (HDDS).

Benchmarks in Hospitality and Tourism

CONTENTS

ABOUT THE EDITOR

Sungsoo Pyo, PhD, is Professor in the Department of Tourism Management at Kyonggi University in Seoul, Korea, and the editor of the *Journal of Quality Assurance in Hospitality & Tourism* (Haworth). He is the author or co-author of four books and over 40 professional articles and has presented numerous papers at seminars. Dr. Pyo is on the editorial boards of five journals, including the *Journal of Travel & Tourism Marketing* and *Tourism Analysis*. He is President of Tourism Systems and Quality Management Research Association in Korea, and the editor of the *Journal of Tourism Systems and Quality Management*, published by the Association. In addition, he is the recipient of the Sosung Award for Academic Excellence, awarded by the President of Kyonggi University (1997) and the Outstanding Service Award from the International Management Development Association at the Sixth Annual IMDA World Business Congress (1997). Dr. Pyo's current research interests include destination marketing engineering, quantitative analysis and TQM for destination management. Dr. Pyo is a member of AIEST–the International Association of Scientific Experts in Tourism.

∞ ALL HAWORTH HOSPITALITY PRESS
BOOKS AND JOURNALS ARE PRINTED
ON CERTIFIED ACID-FREE PAPER

INTRODUCTION

Benchmarking the Benchmarks

SUMMARY. Concepts and processes of benchmarking are briefly discussed. Studies in this special issue are reviewed, and the future collaborations in the hospitality and tourism sector are suggested to perform better by benchmarking the best practices. *[Article copies available for a fee from The Haworth Document Delivery Service: 1-800-HAWORTH. E-mail address: <getinfo@haworthpressinc.com> Website: <http://www.HaworthPress.com> © 2002 by The Haworth Press, Inc. All rights reserved.]*

KEYWORDS. Benchmarking, case studies, performance, best practices

Benchmarking is the search for the industry best practices that will lead to superior performance (Camp, 1989:68). Benchmarking is one of the learning processes. To perform the benchmarking work, the process should be formalized first, performances should be compared to the industry leaders and performance gaps should be measured and identified, and commitments made to the operational processes to close the gaps (Figure 1). Performance gap analysis is to identify the operations to target for improvements.

[Haworth co-indexing entry note]: "Benchmarking the Benchmarks." Pyo, Sungsoo. Co-published simultaneously in *Journal of Quality Assurance in Hospitality & Tourism* (The Haworth Hospitality Press, an imprint of The Haworth Press, Inc.) Vol. 2, No. 3/4, 2001, pp. 1-5; and: *Benchmarks in Hospitality and Tourism* (ed: Sungsoo Pyo) The Haworth Hospitality Press, an imprint of The Haworth Press, Inc., 2001, pp. 1-5. Single or multiple copies of this article are available for a fee from The Haworth Document Delivery Service [1-800-HAWORTH, 9:00 a.m. - 5:00 p.m. (EST). E-mail address: getinfo@haworthpressinc.com].

FIGURE 1. The Benchmarking Process

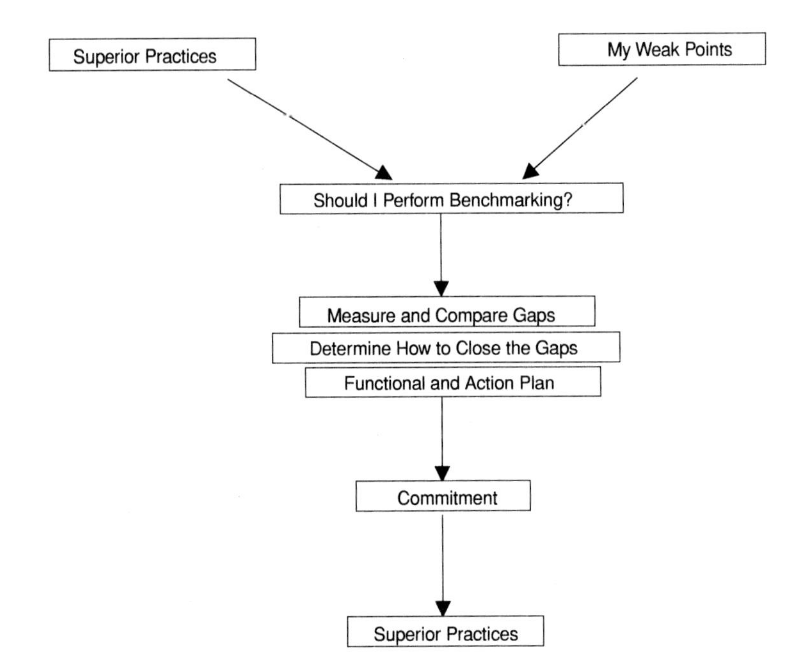

Eight studies are included in this special issue. One paper is about overview of the benchmarking literature, and one paper deals with tourism. Others are concentrated in the hospitality business. Two studies deal with the environmental perspectives.

Metin Kozak and Kevin Nield discuss benchmarking using the related literature. Definitions of the concept, the purpose of benchmarking process, barriers to successful benchmarking, types of benchmarking, analysis of benchmarking models, and evaluation of benchmarking studies in tourism are described.

The second study, conducted by Kurt Matzler and Harald Pechlaner, is about guest satisfaction barometer and benchmarking, which reports experiences from Austria. The implementation of a customer satisfaction barometer facilitates competitive benchmarking and delivers valuable information for quality improvement. The guest satisfaction barometer in Austria was established in 2000. Its objective was to measure guest satisfaction in a systematic and continuous way, to provide participating hotels with information on overall satisfaction, attribute satisfaction, price satisfaction, complaining behavior, loyalty, word-of-mouth, etc., to identify strengths and weaknesses, as well as improving opportunities, and to provide participating hotels with data for competitive benchmarking. According to their experience, a high number of participating hotels, low costs for the participating hotels, data collection and analysis by a neutral institution, standardized questionnaire combined with open-response questions, and fast availability of results are the requirements to be fulfilled in order to benefit from such an initiative.

Karl W. Wöber wrote "A Heuristic Model for Benchmarking SME Hotel and Restaurant Businesses on the Internet" which introduces a heuristic procedure for the identification of benchmarking partners in an interactive database environment on the Internet. The system is based on a weighting model that uses managerial judgements in order to identify similar hotel and restaurant businesses. It enables to compare the performance of hotel and restaurant enterprises with others of a similar nature. In the present paper the author gives a comprehensive description of the conceptual approach, the technical realization and experiences and implications with the system.

"Development Opportunities for a Tourism Benchmarking Tool–The Case of Tyrol," co-authored by Matthias Fuchs and Klaus Weiermair, emphasizes its strategic significance of continually monitoring and emulating standards of performance. The study uses an already-existing benchmarking tool, the Tyrolean Tourism Barometer, and is described in the form of a case study. Both the data gathering process as well as the operational sequence leading to a variety of indicators is thoroughly discussed. The *Tyrolean Tourism Barometer* uses two data inputs. One variable quantifies tourism demand, namely overnight stays and another variable measures corresponding price developments. In order to define structurally similar destination units, the cluster analysis is used. The data are built upon a matrix investigating 278 different Tyrolean tourism communities and 19 cluster-variables to best characterize and distinguish tourism destinations. The paper concludes by analyzing the strengths and weaknesses of this secondary data-based benchmarking tool. The final section of the paper critically assesses the neglect of relevant elements of benchmarking within the production process of tourism services.

"Benchmarking Best Practice in Hotel Front Office: The Western European Experience," co-authored by Tom Baum and Peter Odgers, identifies best practice case examples relating to a variety of different areas of hotel front office operations, work and training. Issues addressed by the research include the operational effects of the flattening of the organization in the front office, the increasing expectation of multi-tasking and multi-skilling, and creating a balance between technological solutions and the delivery of quality customer care. After discussing research objectives and methodologies, benchmarking and best practices in hotel front office, key findings, and implications of study findings for training are delineated, in addition to the needs of the focus of front office work in the next decade.

Vesna Vrtiprah, author of "Managing Quality in Hotel Excelsior." The paper first reviews the importance of quality in hotels. The author mentions that the way to total quality is different for each company, depending upon the desired objectives. However, all companies undergo a similar journey and give importance to the same activities in order to develop a quality that satisfies their targeted market, which is confirmed by case studies. The processes to gain an ISO 9002 registration, which was seen as the avoidance of adopting a five-star mentality from the start, were presented in detail. Management efforts to improve the quality were further discussed. Almost all departments have seen the advantages of ISO registration, and have been successful in delivering a range of products and services that customers want in an efficient and effective way. There is some evidence of ISO 9002's contribution to cost effectiveness.

David Leslie, author of "Serviced Accommodation, Environmental Performance and Benchmarks," suggests that environmental indicators for tourism enterprises should consider three dimensions of sustainable development, to introduce the benchmarks in the industry: the local economy, environment and the community. The indicators may include profile of the accommodation operations, awareness, perceptions and attitudes of owners, staffing, environmental management, purchasing policies, patterns and practices, and guests. Especially, the followings should be emphasized for the successful introduction of benchmarks for environmental performance: ineffectiveness of lead agencies, a weakness of environmental management initiatives, seasonality, community involvement in planning and development, local produce and local products, recycling, visitors–accommodation guests. It is the attitudes and values of the individual–the enterprises' owners–which, combined with their knowledge and understanding of environmental issues and related practices, is the key influence in terms of taking appropriate actions.

Bill Meade and Joe Pringle suggest in their paper, entitled "Environmental Management Systems for Caribbean Hotels and Resorts: A Case Study of Five Properties in Jamaica," that hotels and resorts around the world are now adopting environmental management systems as a means of improving resource use efficiency, reducing operating costs, increasing staff involvement and guest awareness, and obtaining international recognition in the travel and tourism marketplace. This article examines the cost savings and performance improvements at five hotel properties in Jamaica that were among the first in the Caribbean to adopt an environmental management system (EMS). The five hotels evaluated in the case study have achieved remarkable improvements in environmental performance and accompanying cost savings since implementing environmental management systems.

Metin Kozak and Kevin Nield find out that the use of benchmarking in the tourism industry has been very limited and is still in its infancy. It has been restricted to the study of operational units and businesses, rather than destinations. The limited number of benchmarking studies carried out within the tourism industry, and almost all of the benchmarking studies, have been conducted by external third parties. It is apparent that the benchmarking model needs further development. To date, there have been far more conceptual papers on why benchmarking is important and how to operationalize it than empirical research focusing on methodological issues such as how to measure performance gaps. Most empirical studies are based upon the supply side but avoiding the demand side. This special issue fills some of the gaps. However, further collaborative studies in the hospitality and tourism sector are suggested to perform better by benchmarking the best practices.

REFERENCE

Camp, Robert C. January 1989. Benchmarking: The Search for Best Practices that Lead to Superior Performance. *Quality Progress*, pp. 61-68.

Sungsoo Pyo

ARTICLES

An Overview of Benchmarking Literature: Its Strengths and Weaknesses

Metin Kozak
Kevin Nield

SUMMARY. The aim of this paper is to review the concept of benchmarking with emphasis on its strengths and weaknesses and the methods by which it can be applied to tourist facilities and destinations. To achieve its aim, the paper presents several approaches to the benchmarking and benchmarking development. In doing this, it examines the perceived benefits and costs of benchmarking and the implementation process. It then examines the different benchmarking methods using qualitative and quantitative research to identify performance gaps. From this, weaknesses of past benchmarking research are addressed.

Metin Kozak is Lecturer in the School of Tourism and Hotel Management, Mugla University, Turkey.

Kevin Nield is Principal Lecturer/Leader of the Centre for International Hospitality Management, Sheffield Hallam University, City Campus, Sheffield S1 1WB, U.K.

[Haworth co-indexing entry note]: "An Overview of Benchmarking Literature: Its Strengths and Weaknesses." Kozak, Metin, and Kevin Nield. Co-published simultaneously in *Journal of Quality Assurance in Hospitality & Tourism* (The Haworth Hospitality Press, an imprint of The Haworth Press, Inc.) Vol. 2, No. 3/4, 2001, pp. 7-23; and: *Benchmarks in Hospitality and Tourism* (ed: Sungsoo Pyo) The Haworth Hospitality Press, an imprint of The Haworth Press, Inc., 2001, pp. 7-23. Single or multiple copies of this article are available for a fee from The Haworth Document Delivery Service [1-800-HAWORTH, 9:00 a.m. - 5:00 p.m. (EST). E-mail address: getinfo@haworthpressinc.com].

Finally, it analyses the development of benchmarking within the tourism industry together with some examples and its limitations.

KEYWORDS. Benchmarking, quality management, tourism businesses, tourist destinations

INTRODUCTION

Benchmarking basically stems from Deming's quality management theory that aims to enhance quality and check its sustainability. Despite this relative clarity, benchmarking has been defined differently by a variety of organisations and authors even though each aims to reach the same conclusion (Camp 1989; Vaziri 1992; Codling 1992; Watson 1993). Nevertheless, all of these definitions have a common theme, namely, that benchmarking is the continuous measurement and improvement of an organisation's performance against the best in order to obtain information about new working methods or practices in other organisations. As Watson (1993) says, the benchmarking concept should be viewed as a process of adaptation, not adoption. It is not just a question of copying what others are doing, the power in benchmarking comes from sharing ideas. As benchmarking has been considered to be the process of learning from the best practices and experiences of others, some authors have used the term *benchlearning* (e.g., Karlof and Ostblom 1993). Thus, benchmarking is not different from the principle of learning from the experiences of others, but its real use is that it puts this learning experience into a structured framework.

Benchmarking theory is simply based on performance comparison, gap identification and the change management process (Watson 1993). A review of benchmarking literature shows that many of the benchmarking methods perform the same functions as performance gap analysis (e.g., Camp 1989; Watson 1993; Karlof and Ostblom 1993). The rule in benchmarking is firstly to identify performance gaps with respect to production and consumption within the organisation and then to develop methods to close them. The gap between internal and external practices reveals which changes, if any, are necessary. It is this feature that differentiates benchmarking theory from comparison research and competitive analysis. Some researchers have made the mistake of believing that every comparison survey is a form of benchmarking. Competitive analysis seeks product or service comparisons but benchmarking goes beyond comparison and assesses the operating and management skills that produce these products and services. It is also different in that competitive analysis only looks at characteristics of those in the same geographic area of competition whilst benchmarking seeks to find the best practices regardless of location (Walleck, O'Halloran and Leader 1991).

Upon reviewing an extensive selection of literature (e.g., Camp 1989; Zairi 1992; Rogers, Daugherty and Stank 1995), it is apparent that the purposes of benchmarking are to:

- help businesses understand where they have strengths and weaknesses depending upon changes in supply, demand and market conditions.
- help better satisfy the customer's needs for quality, cost, product and service by establishing new standards and goals.
- motivate employees to reach new standards and to welcome new developments within the related area and to improve the motivation of employees.
- allow businesses to realise what level(s) of performance is achievable by considering other methods and to show how such improvement may be made.
- document reasons as to why these differences exist.
- enable businesses to improve their competitive advantage by stimulating continuous improvement in order to maintain world-class performance and increase competitive standards.
- establish a pool of innovative ideas that are cost-effective and time-efficient from which the most applicable examples may be utilised.

Despite these benefits, several barriers to successful benchmarking exist. Barriers identified include time constraints, competitive barriers, cost, lack of management commitment and professional human resources, resistance to change, poor planning and short-term expectations (Bendell, Boulter and Kelly 1993). A poorly-executed benchmarking exercise will result in a waste of financial and human resources as well as time. Ineffectively-executed benchmarking projects may have tarnished an organisation's image (Elmuti and Kathawala 1997).

The result of this is that there are risks involved in benchmarking others and in adopting new standards into the own organisation. 'Best practice' should be perceived or accepted to be amongst those practices producing superior outcomes and being judged as good examples within the area. One final criticism is that benchmarking findings may remove the heterogeneity of an industry because practices will themselves become globally standardised and attempts to produce differentiation may fail (Cox and Thompson 1998). For these reasons, benchmarking has its detractors, indeed Campbell (1999) suggests that businesses should spend little time on benchmarking, instead they should focus on their own planning procedures with regard to their own needs.

TYPES OF BENCHMARKING

Several classifications of benchmarking are recorded in the literature. The main categorisations are internal, competitive, functional and generic benchmarking (Camp 1989; Zairi 1992). For ease of use the literature may be divided into two parts: internal and external benchmarking. In this context, competitive, functional and generic benchmarking will be classed under external benchmarking. Each is briefly explained below:

- *Internal benchmarking* covers two-way communication and sharing opinions between departments within the same organisation or between organisations operating as part of a chain in different countries (Cross and Leonard 1994; Breiter and Kliner 1995). Once any part of an organisation has a better performance indicator, others can learn how this was achieved. Findings of internal benchmarking can then be used as a baseline for extending benchmarking to include external organisations (McNair and Leibfried 1992). Advantages of internal benchmarking are the ability to deal with partners who share a common language, culture and systems and having easy access to data (Cook 1995). However, it is claimed that this type of benchmarking study is time-consuming and potentially wasteful, as competitors could be busy increasing their market share while the sample organisation is busy measuring its internal performance (Cook 1995).
- *Competitive benchmarking* refers to a comparison with direct competitors only. This is accepted as the most sensitive type of benchmarking as it is very difficult to achieve a healthy collaboration and co-operation with direct competitors and reach primary sources of information. As a result, this type of benchmarking is believed to be more rational for larger businesses than smaller ones (Cook 1995).
- *Functional benchmarking* refers to comparative research carried out not only against competitors but also of those who are not in direct competition, but operating in similar fields and performing similar activities (Karlof and Ostblom 1993). For instance, British Rail Network South East employed a benchmarking process to improve the standard of cleanliness on trains. British Airways was selected as a partner because a team of 11 people cleans a 250-seat Jumbo aircraft in only nine minutes. After the benchmarking exercise, a team of 10 people were able to clean a

660-seat train in eight minutes (Cook 1995). This type of benchmarking is also known as non-competitive benchmarking.

- *Generic benchmarking* attempts to seek world-class excellence by comparing business performance not only against competitors but also against the best businesses operating in similar fields and performing similar activities or those having similar problems but in a different industry (Breiter and Kliner 1995). Therefore, a hotel organisation's accounting department could look at the accounting department of a manufacturing organisation that has been identified as having the fastest operations. It is believed to be easier to obtain data in such arrangements as best-in-class organisations are more likely to share their experiences. The disadvantages of generic benchmarking are that it can take a long time to complete and research outcomes may need a lot of modification in order for organisations to set their own standards (Cook 1995).
- Andersen (1995) introduces a further type of external benchmarking called 'relationship benchmarking' which refers to benchmarking against an organisation with whom the benchmarker already had a relationship in advance of a benchmarking agreement. This method may potentially provide some benefits to organisations since less time is required and the trust established between the two parties will help break down confidentiality barriers. Relationship benchmarking which was introduced as an alternative option to 'competitive benchmarking' is also known as 'collaborative benchmarking' (Cox, Mann and Samson 1997).

ANALYSIS OF BENCHMARKING MODELS

Benchmarking method requires two parties, the benchmarker and the benchmarkee. The former is the organisation carrying out a benchmarking procedure whereas the latter is the organisation being benchmarked. Although benchmarking theory has been derived from Deming's four stages: *plan*, *do*, *check* and *act,* numerous benchmarking process models have been proposed by researchers both in industry and academia. Approximately forty different models have been identified that originate from individual organisations, consulting agencies and individual researchers. The number of phases and process steps in these models is variable. While some specify five phases consisting of a total of fourteen steps (e.g., Camp 1989; Karlof and Ostblom 1993), some have just four phases with the same number of steps (e.g., Watson 1993).

Having reviewed all the major models, the steps of planning, data collection, analysis, action, and review may be postulated as the main categorisation. The benchmarking process should begin in the host organisation in order to be able to specify areas that need to be measured (Camp 1989; Vaziri 1992; Watson 1993). Further steps are then to collect data, examine gaps between partners to identify strengths and weaknesses, take action and review the future performance level of the host organisation. The review stage enables the organisation to understand whether or not the process has achieved its objectives.

The traditional benchmarking approach refers to the notion that there must be a gap between the host and the partner. The gap analysis model considers the differences between performance levels of businesses. The standard to be set is that the higher value is the best practice. For example, when the scores for two businesses A (the benchmarker) and B (the benchmarkee) are compared, if the score is greater than zero, it is strength for business A and a weakness for business B. This is regarded as a positive gap. On the other hand, when the score is less than zero (negative), this means that the specific attribute performs better in business B than business A. This is regarded as a negative gap. A large negative gap could be an indicator that radical change is required. The results of this research will determine whether benchmarking research needs to be carried out.

It should be noted that it is the fact that a performance gap can also be neutral indicating no identifiable difference between compared attributes (Kozak, 2000). The gap exists as a result of differences in performance. Only past and present gaps can be known or measured. In the early stages of benchmarking, most gaps are supposed to be negative. When progress is recorded, the gap begins to decrease. Targeted future performance must be greater than the partner's. However, partners are more likely to increase their performance levels even without benchmarking as they gain greater industry experience and infrastructure (Codling 1992). Hence, the benchmarker needs to record a significant improvement initially towards their targets and then to close the gap.

THE ORGANISATION OF A BENCHMARKING EXERCISE

Benchmarking literature demonstrates that there are two main approaches to carrying out benchmarking, i.e., it is either self administered or conducted by a third party/research group. In a self-administered benchmarking approach, businesses benchmark their performance levels against others and learn about the best practices for their operations e.g., competitive benchmarking. In a third-party benchmarking approach, research groups and national and international benchmarking organisations (or consultants) such as the European Foundation for Quality Management (EFQM), the Confederation of British Industry (CBI), UK Department of Trade Industry (DTI) and Benchmarking Clearinghouse measure the performance of a business individually or of an industry as a whole.

Selected businesses are included in the process and the best and worst performance indicators are ranked respectively. On the basis of these results, experts or organisations present their recommendations and action plans. A few organisations such as the US Benchmarking Clearinghouse and the UK Department of Trade and Industry have launched a network for organisations that want to compare their performance levels (on the basis of different indicators) against that of similar organisations. Clearinghouse services include networking, information, partner identification, training and databases of past research. Small businesses may also need the support of consultancy organisations that are experts in benchmarking. Research-based benchmarking studies in academia, like this present research, can also be considered within the category of third party benchmarking methodology.

This type of classification may also illustrate the boundaries of time when a benchmarking research project is conducted. When benchmarking projects are done by third party professional organisations, the benchmarking research will be defined as a singular activity, start with a specific date and have a specific completion date. As far as a self-administered benchmarking is concerned, businesses do not have to limit themselves to particular time periods. They can self-administer benchmarking projects as a continuous activity in order to keep up-to-date with developments in relevant areas (Spendolini 1992). Research findings indicate that some US businesses are repeating benchmarking studies every two to five years (Bendell et al. 1993).

EVALUATING BENCHMARKING STUDIES IN TOURISM

It is usual within the literature that studies of benchmarking within the tourism industry involve hotels (Codling 1992; Canon and Kent 1994; Breiter and Kliner 1995; CBI News 1995; Morey and Dittmann 1995; Barsky 1996; Department of National Heritage 1996; Struebing 1996; Johns, Lee-Ross, Graves and Ingram 1996; Johns, Lee-Ross and Ingram 1997; Min and Min 1997; Phillips and Appiah-Adu 1998). The benchmarking approach has been further extended to visitor attractions. Tourist attractions such as HMS Victory, the Tower of London and Dover Castle were benchmarked (Cheshire 1997). More recent benchmarking studies have concerned tourist destinations. In this context, several organisations have directed their attention towards carrying out destination benchmarking research which is primarily applicable for practical purposes (European Commission 1998; Thomason, Colling and Wyatt 1999a, b).

The majority of the aforementioned studies focused on the assessment of customer satisfaction as a qualitative demand side measure of performance in identifying strengths and weaknesses of businesses (Barsky 1996; Morey and

Dittmann 1995; Department of National Heritage 1996; Johns et al. 1996, 1997; Min and Min 1997). In addition, there is a smaller number of examples of research on the supply side using quantitative measures such as occupancy rates, cost, revenues and capital investment (Breiter and Kliner 1995; CBI News 1995; Morey and Dittmann 1995).

Thus far, the use of benchmarking in the tourism industry has been very limited and is still in its infancy. It has been restricted to the study of operational units and businesses, rather than destinations. It is significant and interesting to note that the limited examples of benchmarking carried out within the tourism industry almost all involve the benchmarking process being carried out by external third parties. Both quantitative and qualitative measures were used collecting data from questionnaire surveys, secondary sources and observations. There is a limited number of benchmarking studies in tourism solely focusing on measuring the performance of tourist facilities or destinations and providing methods to improve it. The weaknesses of benchmarking research in the tourism and hospitality industry also apply to the context of benchmarking in general. In the light of these observations, it is apparent that the benchmarking model needs further development.

To date, there have been far more conceptual papers on why benchmarking is important and how to operationalise it than empirical research focusing on methodological issues such as how to measure performance gaps. As indicated in Table 1, the overwhelming majority of researchers preferred establishing an empirical study based upon the supply side but avoiding the demand side. Whilst this table is not a complete list of the research in the field, it is indicative of the fact that there is diversity in respect of sampling choice, types of benchmarking, use of quantitative or qualitative measures, considering cross-cultural differences and use of statistical tools. We will now turn our attention to addressing the several weaknesses in the past studies of benchmarking tourist facilities or destinations.

Benchmarking Is Not Solely a Comparison Activity

Within the tourism literature, there is a growing body of research assuming that benchmarking is solely a comparison activity (Breiter and Kliner 1995; Min and Min 1997; Meyer et al. 1999). As has been already-stated comparison is only one stage of benchmarking (performance gap analysis). Other stages such as taking action and reviewing outcomes in order to improve performance may be more significant. The stage of taking action is possibly one of the most difficult parts of the benchmarking process, as local authorities, tourism organisations and businesses may not intend to implement findings or to take long-term decisions. This may be due to lack of human or financial re-

TABLE 1. Overview of Past Benchmarking Research

Authors	Sampling	Types of Industry	Types of Benchmarking	Quantitative or Qualitative Measures	Cultural Implications (Supply)	Cultural Implications (Demand)	Gap Analysis
Thomason, Colling and Wyatt 1999a	Customers	UK Destinations	Internal (comparison with previous years)	Qualitative (Likert scale)	N/A	No	Yes
Thomason, Colling and Wyatt 1999b	Customers	UK Destinations	External	Qualitative (Likert scale)	No	No	Yes
Boger, Lai and Lin 1999	Organisations	US Hotels	External	Quantitative (metrics such as room rates)	No	N/A	Yes
European Commission 1998	Destinations	European Destinations	Internal	Case studies	No	No	N/A
Phillips and Appiah-Adu 1998	Organisations	UK Hotels	External	Qualitative (Likert scale)	No	N/A	Yes
Min and Min 1997	Organisations & Customers	Korean Hotels	External	Qualitative (Likert scale)	No	No	Yes
Johns, Lee-Ross, Moris and Ingram 1996	Customers	UK Hotels	External & Internal	Qualitative (free-response survey)	No	No	Yes
Department of National Heritage 1996	Organisations & Customers	UK Hotels	Generic	Qualitative (scoring)	No	No	N/A
Breiter and Kliner 1995	Organisations	US Hotels	External	Qualitative (Likert scale)	No	N/A	Yes
Morey and Dittman 1995	Organisations	US Hotels	External	Quantitative (costs) and qualitative	No	No	Yes
Bell and Morey 1995	Organisations	US Travel Industry	External	Quantitative (costs and expenses)	No	N/A	Yes

Source: Own elaboration from the literature review.

sources and the sensitivity of the tourism industry to economic, political and social changes. The establishment of action plans may also be influenced by cross-cultural differences in managerial practices, beliefs and values between peer organisations or destinations in the case of external benchmarking. This issue also applies to the consideration of cross-cultural differences between tourist groups in the case of either internal or external benchmarking.

The Importance of Customer Satisfaction in Benchmarking

Little has been done with regard to the empirical assessment of customer satisfaction as a performance assessment and improvement tool although benchmarking literature has highlighted its significance in benchmarking process (e.g., Johns et al. 1996; Thomason et al. 1999a). The majority of benchmarking studies have focused upon the investigation of the establishment of best performance practices and areas from the supply side by using qualitative or quantitative measures of one organisation and comparing them with another (e.g., Bell and Morey 1994; Edgett and Snow 1996; Zairi 1998; Boger, Lai and Lin 1999).

Competitiveness is the key element of management and marketing strategy, therefore long-range planning and customer satisfaction could be the two major objectives of tourism businesses and tourist destinations. The concepts of performance and satisfaction are strongly interrelated as the level of product or service performance brings satisfaction. As a result, Bogan and English (1994) argue that customer-service performance measures should include satisfaction, dissatisfaction, retention and defection benchmarks. The last two are included as they represent the customers' future intentions. It is claimed that:

> Customer satisfaction is a major benefit to be gained from benchmarking. It allows organizations to adopt helicopter vision and helps prevent complacency through developing the discipline of focusing externally. (Cook 1995:29-30)

It is therefore further suggested that feedback received from customers is a suitable way of comparing the performance of an organisation (or destination) to that of another (Kotler 1994). The availability of alternative service providers (e.g., competitor destinations) appears to be significant in influencing the level of customer satisfaction since customers have a tendency to compare one service encounter with another (Czepiel, Rosenberg and Akerele 1974). The level of customer satisfaction may have a pivotal role not only in identifying the current position but also in designing future performance and highlighting where there is a need for further improvement. According to customers, the performance level of facilities or destinations is based on mostly qualitative measures, e.g., the extent to which it provides a satisfactory service or it has a favourable image in the market (Morrison 1989; Um and Crompton 1990). These measures may then be used to make a comparison between facilities or destinations to determine which one performs better than the others. The outcome of this assessment could impact on their future behaviour of returning to or recommending destinations.

Heterogeneous Structure of Customers

Benchmarking studies ensure that customers visiting different organisations or destinations are homogeneous in terms of their socio-demographic and socio-economic characteristics as well as in terms of motivations, purchasing behaviour and loyalty. However, this is unlikely, in other words, one customer group shopping from one organisation will not necessarily be in the same category as another shopping at a different organisation. This argument has been underestimated within the benchmarking literature. Using an example from a destination benchmarking study, it is not reasonable to expect that tourists visiting Italy are the same as those visiting Greece or that both destinations attract similar markets.

In external benchmarking, it is important to identify any difference in the characteristics of the sample population visiting destinations. This type of assessment is helpful for identifying not only the profile of market segments but also partner destinations with whom external benchmarking is to be conducted. Such research may be significant for tourism benchmarking research in order to have a better understanding of competitors involved in the same set in terms of a particular market and make a decision about whom and what to benchmark. As an example for destination benchmarking, the Mediterranean destinations could select their benchmarking partners from countries in the Mediterranean basin because the majority of tourists in Western European countries tend to take their summer holidays in this region.

Significance of Internal and Generic Benchmarking

A considerable amount of research has been carried out dealing with the application of external benchmarking comparing one organisation's or destination's performance to that of others (e.g., Morey and Dittmann 1995; Min and Min 1997; Thomason et al. 1999b). By contrast, little research has been carried out to develop methodologies for internal or generic benchmarking studies. Some of those who studied internal benchmarking compared findings to those of previous years (e.g., Thomason et al. 1999a). Of those that followed generic benchmarking guidelines, some attempted to establish best practices within the industry based on performance scores marked by both consultants and customers (Department of National Heritage 1996). Despite this, both internal and generic types of benchmarking seem worthy of further investigation in tourism studies.

In today's multi-functional and multi-cultural world, some businesses or destinations may have their own cultural, economic and political characteristics which have limited application to transfer to others or cannot easily be revised by looking at others. Examples of this are hospitality, harassment, low currency exchange values, and tourist and visa regulations in a country (Kozak, 2000). These variables may be measurable and compatible but are not comparable for external benchmarking purposes. The strength of internal benchmarking is that it helps to find the methods that are relevant to a particular culture and practices and build up local strategies on the basis of the characteristics of the managerial and social culture and specific objectives. There is no need to spend time in collecting data from others and observing their performance levels. The main purpose of internal benchmarking is to improve the performance of tourism businesses or tourist destinations by identifying their own strengths and weaknesses on the basis of the feedback obtained from travellers and the local population.

Existing literature emphasises that the core idea of benchmarking is to identify the best practices or the best performing businesses in the industry and improve one's own performance by adapting good practices used by others or guidelines established by professional national or international organisations (Evans and Lindsey 1993; Zairi 1996). Consistent with this, within the application of generic benchmarking, businesses or destinations in tourism can be advised to look either at others or international standards in order to find effective solutions for their particular problems by having access to best practices recognised nationally or internationally. For example, complaints about service quality and environmental deregulation might not be limited to particular hotel businesses or tourist destinations. Methods of improving these attributes could be modified to be used internationally, e.g., use of quality grading and eco-labelling systems. This study suggests that various quality grading and eco-label systems act as external enablers, as a form of generic benchmarking, that influence the performance of tourist facilities or holiday destinations.

Cross-Cultural Differences

Previous studies have not paid much attention to the consideration of cross-cultural differences either between organisations or between customer groups. The existence of such differences in organisation and national culture, and in customer groups from different cultural backgrounds may impact upon the transferability of findings and the success of their implementation into the host organisation. Marketing literature confirms the existence of cross-cultural differences in attitude and perceptions between customers from different countries (e.g., Richardson and Crompton 1988; Armstrong, Mok, Go and Chan 1997). It is our contention that this issue requires serious consideration in future benchmarking research.

While setting goals and establishing action plans, destination management can benefit from the findings of either internal or external benchmarking exercises depending upon which one has been followed. In the case of external benchmarking, methods used by other destinations and thought to be rational and applicable to one's own purposes can be considered. Attention needs to be paid to the factors that affect the success of practices and the overall performance of benchmarking studies, e.g., cultural differences between tourist-receiving and tourist-generating countries, and between different tourist-receiving countries. Types of customers visiting different destinations, the power of marketing channels and their restructuring, and differences in managerial practices and services between tourist-receiving countries are also the subject of benchmarking research in tourism.

There is no single best practice that can bring about performance improvement and help gain competitive advantage. The selection of measures depends on the aims and objectives of each authority. Different businesses or destinations might have different objectives and expectations from the tourism industry. For instance, some destinations offer a variety of tourist facilities and activities and are year-round destinations that attract top-class customer groups, while others offer only seasonal facilities and services for middle or low-income customer groups. As a result, the rationale for measuring performance differs from one to another. One destination might use it to increase customer satisfaction and subsequently raise the volume of arrivals or tourism receipts. Another may think that it is an effective method of having a sustainable form of tourism development within the area, despite fewer tourists or a lower tourism income.

Another point to be taken into account in tourism benchmarking research is that facilities or tourist destinations attract customers from different cultures and countries; therefore it is not reasonable to examine the variables of only one group of customers and take action in line with the feedback. Those who come from other main generating countries should also be included in this type of analysis. The findings of past tourism benchmarking research confirmed the existence of differences in tourists' motivation, satisfaction, expenditure and the number of previous visits (Kozak 2000). For example, the level of the spoken and written language at the destination may be very good for one group, but it may not seem so to those who speak another language. This study, therefore, suggests undertaking a separate benchmarking exercise for each national group. This type of analysis may assist authorities to establish their positioning strategies and explore their core competencies for each group. It may also assist in investigating reasons for differences between customer groups and enabling the establishment of effective strategies for improvement.

CONCLUSION

This paper has given an overview of benchmarking theory and its implications for performance improvement in tourism businesses or tourist destinations. In doing this, it has reviewed both the concept of benchmarking and its methods of application. It has examined and critiqued the main approaches to benchmarking and in the course of doing it has indicated the weaknesses and the strengths of each.

The paper has specifically examined the use of benchmarking in tourism and concludes that research in this area is limited. Past research in this area has tended to concentrate upon conceptual ideas such has why benchmarking is important and how benchmarking may be operationalised rather than empirical research focusing on methodological issues such as how to measure performance gaps. As a result of this, the paper has demonstrated that there are several weaknesses (limitations) in past studies of tourism benchmarking that need to be addressed. From our survey of the literature it is apparent that the major gap in the literature is that there is little experience of putting benchmarking theory into practice.

The literature survey enables us to point out the major criticisms of previous benchmarking studies. In summary, these are as follows.

1. The literature has been almost solely comparative. This has led to the omission of other important stages of the benchmarking process such as taking action and reviewing outcomes.
2. The tourism benchmarking literature has made little use of empirical assessments of customer satisfaction as a benchmark for performance.
3. In tourism benchmarking the need for homogeneity has been underestimated.
4. Little work has been carried out with regard to methodologies for internal or generic benchmarking studies. These studies may be as important as external benchmarking studies.
5. More attention must be paid to the consideration of cross-cultural differences that exist between customer groups; organisations and tourist destinations.

In conclusion it is our contention that if benchmarking is to be further applied to tourism, the weaknesses that have been identified must be addressed to seek to ensure that it is valid, accurate and useable.

REFERENCES

Andersen, B. (1995). "Benchmarking in Norwegian Industry and Relationship Benchmarking." In *Benchmarking: Theory and Practice*, edited by A. Rolstadas. London: Chapman-Hall, pp.105-109.

Armstrong, R. W., C. Mok, F. Go, and G. Chan (1997). "The Importance of Cross-cultural Expectations in the Measurement of Service Quality Perceptions in the Hotel Industry." *International Journal of Hospitality Management*, 16(2):181-190.

Barsky, J. D. (1996). "Building a Program for World-Class Service." *Cornell Hotel and Restaurant Administration Quarterly*. February: 17-27.

Bell, R., and R. Morey (1994). "The Search for Appropriate Benchmarking Partners: A Macro Approach and Application to Corporate Travel Management." *Omega*, 22(5):477-490.

Bendell, T., L. Boulter, and J. Kelly (1993). *Benchmarking for Competitive Advantage*. London: Financial Times-Pitman Publishing.

Bogan, C. E., and M. J. English (1994). *Benchmarking for Best Practices: Winning through Innovative Adaptation*. New York: McGraw-Hill.

Boger, C. A., L. A. Cai, and L. Li (1999). "Benchmarking: Comparing Discounted Business Rates among Lodging Companies." *Journal of Hospitality and Tourism Research*, 23(3):256-267.

Breiter, D., and S. F. Kliner (1995). "Benchmarking Quality Management in Hotels." *FIU Hospitality Review*, 13(2):45-52.

Camp, R. C. (1989). *Benchmarking: The Search for Industry Best Practices that Leads to Superior Performance*. ASQC Quality Press.

Campbell, A. (1999). "Tailored, Not Benchmarked: A Fresh Look at Corporate Planning." *Harvard Business Review*, March-April:41-50.

Canon, D. F., and W. E. Kent (1994). "What Every Hospitality Educator Should Know about Benchmarking." *Hospitality and Tourism Educator*, 6(4):61-64.

CBI News (1995). "Room for Improvement in Britain's Hotel Sector." November-December, p.24.

Cheshire, M. (1997). "Introducing the Concept of Best Practice Benchmarking into the Portsmouth Heritage Area." *Tourism*, Summer:6-7

Codling, S. (1992). *Best Practice Benchmarking: A Management Guide*. Hampshire: Gower.

Cook, S. (1995). *Practical Benchmarking: A Manager's Guide to Creating a Competitive Advantage*. London: Kogan Page.

Cox, J. R., L. Mann, and D. Samson (1997). "Benchmarking as a Mixed Metaphor: Disentangling Assumptions of Competition and Collaboration." *Journal of Management Studies*, 34(2):285-314.

Cox, A., and I. Thompson (1998). "On the Appropriateness of Benchmarking." *Journal of General Management*, 23(3):1-20.

Cross, R., and P. Leonard (1994). "Benchmarking: A Strategic and Tactical Perspective." In *Managing Quality*, edited by B.G.Dale. Second Edition, Prentice Hall, pp.497-513.

Czepiel, J. A., L. J. Rosenberg, and A. Akerele (1974). "Perspectives on Consumer Satisfaction." In *1974 Combined Proceedings Series No: 36*, edited by R. C. Curhan. American Marketing Association, pp. 119-123.

Department of National Heritage (1996). *Benchmarking for Smaller Hotels: Competing with the Best*. London.

Edgett, S., and K. Snow (1996). "Benchmarking Measures of Customer Satisfaction, Quality and Performance for New Financial Service Products." *The Journal of Services Marketing*, 10(6):6-17.

Elmuti, D., and Y. Kathawala (1997). "An Overview of Benchmarking Process: A Tool for Continuous Improvement and Competitive Advantage." *Benchmarking for Quality Management and Technology*, 4(4):229-243.

European Commission (1998). "Research in the Field of Integrated Quality Management of Tourism Destinations." Http://www.wttc.org. (14 November).

Evans, J. R., and W. M. Lindsey (1993). *The Management and Control of Quality*. (Second Edition). West Publishing Company.

Johns, N., D. Lee-Ross, M. R. Graves, and H. Ingram (1996). "Quality Benchmarking in the Small Hotel Sector Using Profile Accumulation: A New Measurement Tool." *Proceedings of the Fifth Annual Hospitality Research Conference*, Nottingham, 10-11 April, pp.192-207.

Johns, N., D. Lee-Ross, and H. Ingram (1997). "A Study of Service Quality in Small Hotels and Guesthouses." *Progress in Hospitality and Tourism Research*, 3(4):351-363.

Karlof, B., and S. Ostblom (1993). *Benchmarking: A Signpost Excellence in Quality and Productivity*. West Sussex: Wiley.

Kotler, P. (1994). *Marketing Management: Analysis, Planning, Implementation and Control*. Eighth Edition, New Jersey: Prentice Hall International Editions.

Kozak, M. (2000). *Destination Benchmarking: Facilities, Customer Satisfaction and Levels of Tourist Expenditure*, Unpublished PhD Thesis, Sheffield Hallam University, UK.

McNair, C. J., and K. H. J. Leibfried (1992). *Benchmarking: A Tool for Continuous Improvement*. New York: Harper Business.

Meyer, A., R. Chase, A. Roth, C. Voss, K. Sperl, L. Menor, and K. Blackmon (1999). "Service Competitiveness: An International Benchmarking Comparison of Service Practice and Performance in Germany, UK and USA." *International Journal of Service Industry Management*, 10(4):369-379.

Min, H., and H. Min (1997). "Benchmarking the Quality of Hotel Services: Managerial Perspectives." *International Journal of Quality and Reliability Management*, 14(6):582-597.

Morey, R. C., and D. A. Dittman (1995). "Evaluating a Hotel GM's Performance." *Cornell Hotel and Restaurant Administration Quarterly*, October:30-35

Morrison, A. M. (1989). *Hospitality and Travel Marketing*. New York: Albany.

Phillips, P., and K. Appiah-Adu (1998). "Benchmarking to Improve the Strategic Planning Process in the Hotel Sector." *The Service Industries Journal*, 18(1):1-17.

Richardson, S. L., and J. Crompton (1988). "Vacation Patterns of French and English Canadians." *Annals of Tourism Research*, 15(4):430-448.

Rogers, D. S., P. J. Daugherty, and T. P. Stank (1995). "Benchmarking Programs: Opportunities for Enhancing Performance." *Journal of Business Logistics*, 10(2): 43-63.

Spendolini, M. J. (1992). *The Benchmarking Book*. New York: American Management Association.

Struebing, L. (1996). "Measuring for Excellence." *Quality Progress*, December:25-28.

Thomason, L., P. Colling, and C. Wyatt (1999a). "Benchmarking: An Essential Tool in Destination Management and the Achievement of Best Value."*Insights*, January: A111-A117.

Thomason, L., P. Colling, and C. Wyatt (1999b). "Destination Benchmarking II: The 1998 Pilot." *Insights*, May: A173-A180.

Um, S., and J. L. Crompton (1990). "Attitude Determinants in Tourism Destination Choice." *Annals of Tourism Research*, 17:432-448.

Vaziri, K. (1992). "Using Competitive Benchmarking to Set Goals." *Quality Progress*, October: 81-85.

Walleck, A. S., J. D. O'Halloran, and C. A. Leader (1991). "Benchmarking World-Class Performance." *The McKinsey Quarterly*, 1(1):3-24.

Watson G. H. (1993). *Strategic Benchmarking: How to Rate Your Company's Performance against the World's Best*. Canada: Wiley.

Zairi, M. (1992). "The Art of Benchmarking: Using Customer Feedback to Establish a Performance Gap." *Total Quality Management*, 3(2):177-188.

Zairi, M. (1996). *Benchmarking for Best Practice: Continuous Learning through Sustainable Innovation*. Oxford: Butterworth-Heinemann.

Zairi, M. (1998). "Benchmarking at TNT Express." *Benchmarking for Quality Management and Technology*, 5(2):138-149.

Guest Satisfaction Barometer and Benchmarking: Experiences from Austria

Kurt Matzler
Harald Pechlaner

SUMMARY. An increasing number of companies use customer satisfaction data for improvement programs, strategic decision making, and compensation schemes. Typically, single companies carry out satisfaction measurement for their own purposes. As a consequence, results are not comparable with other companies. Thus, valuable information on competition is not available and benchmarking is not possible. Moreover, in order to use satisfaction data for decision-making, it should be measured continuously and systematically. In practice, however, many firms do not have the required resources or competencies to carry out these research activities on their own. As a result, there is a lack of reliable data. The implementation of a customer satisfaction barometer seems to be a promising approach. It facilitates competitive benchmarking and delivers valuable information for quality improvement.

The authors of this paper report their experiences with a guest satisfaction barometer in Austria that was established in 2000. Its objective was (1) to measure guest satisfaction in a systematic and continuous way; (2) to

Kurt Matzler is Associate Professor, Department of Management, Tourism and Service Economics, University of Innsbruck/Austria and visiting scholar at Bocconi University, Milan/Italy.

Harald Pechlaner is Assistant Professor, Department of Management, Tourism and Service Economics, University of Innsbruck/Austria.

[Haworth co-indexing entry note]: "Guest Satisfaction Barometer and Benchmarking: Experiences from Austria." Matzler, Kurt, and Harald Pechlaner. Co-published simultaneously in *Journal of Quality Assurance in Hospitality & Tourism* (The Haworth Hospitality Press, an imprint of The Haworth Press, Inc.) Vol. 2, No. 3/4, 2001, pp. 25-47; and: *Benchmarks in Hospitality and Tourism* (ed: Sungsoo Pyo) The Haworth Hospitality Press, an imprint of The Haworth Press, Inc., 2001, pp. 25-47. Single or multiple copies of this article are available for a fee from The Haworth Document Delivery Service [1-800-HAWORTH, 9:00 a.m. - 5:00 p.m. (EST). E-mail address: getinfo@haworthpressinc.com].

provide participating hotels with information on overall satisfaction, attribute satisfaction, price satisfaction, complaining behavior, loyalty, word-of-mouth, etc.; (3) to identify strengths and weaknesses, as well as improving opportunities; and (4) to provide participating hotels with data for competitive benchmarking. Thirty-seven hotels participated in the pilot phase and data from more than 3,500 guests were collected. In order to illustrate the ideas of the guest satisfaction barometer and the benefits for the participating hotels, the authors first describe the basic ideas and guiding principles of the barometer and report some empirical findings to demonstrate how benchmarks can be used to improve quality and satisfaction. The paper closes with a summary of the experiences and some recommendations for future applications.

KEYWORDS. Customer satisfaction barometer, benchmarking, loyalty, complaining behavior, customer value analysis, importance-performance-analysis

INTRODUCTION

Without question, service quality and customer satisfaction are key drivers of financial performance. It is argued that satisfaction leads to increased loyalty, reduced price elasticity, increased cross-buying, and positive word-of-mouth (e.g., Reichheld and Sasser, 1990; Anderson, Fornell, and Lehmann, 1994; Zeithaml, 2000).

Hence, customer satisfaction management has become a key issue. Many firms track some form of customer satisfaction measure. This data is then used for a wide variety of purposes such as strategic decision-making, improvement programs, and compensation schemes.

In their quest for improved quality and enhanced customer satisfaction, managers often face the following problems.

(1) *Guest satisfaction is not measured in a systematic and regular way:* To be able to interpret and effectively utilize customer satisfaction ratings, it is necessary to collect data systematically and regularly. In practice, however, there often is a lack of consistent and regularly collected information. As a result, it is difficult to monitor changes and to evaluate the effectiveness of improvement programs.

(2) *Key drivers of satisfaction and causes of dissatisfaction are not identified:* Continuous monitoring of customer satisfaction should not only reveal information about overall satisfaction and attribute satisfaction on standardized scales, but should also identify critical incidents that caused satisfaction or dissatisfaction. Only then are the detailed causes of satisfaction and dissatisfaction understood, and specific measures can be taken.

(3) *Competitor information is not available:* In order to deliver higher quality and create superior value for the customer, one needs to assess satisfaction relative to competitors. This allows a company to identify strengths and weaknesses as well as improvement areas. Unfortunately, accurate competitor information is rarely available. Its collection is costly and time consuming and in many cases companies have to rely on vague and incomplete benchmarks.

(4) *Results are not available timely:* When quality problems occur, it is crucial to react promptly. Therefore, customer satisfaction ratings must be available immediately. In many cases however, results of satisfaction measurements are not available timely and their usefulness is limited.

In summary, customer satisfaction measurement should be done systematically and regularly, drivers of satisfaction and dissatisfaction should be identified, competitor information should be assessed and results should be available timely.

In this paper, the authors demonstrate how these requirements can be fulfilled using data from a guest satisfaction barometer that was established in the Alpine region of Austria in 2000. One of the biggest shortcomings of traditional satisfaction measurement is the lack of information about competitors, and consequently the missing benchmark opportunities. It will be shown that such a guest satisfaction barometer provides useful information on competitors, making it a helpful tool for benchmarking.

Benchmarking at the company level also plays an important role for destinations as a whole. Directly or indirectly, guest satisfaction for a destination's service element (e.g., facilities and infrastructure) is influencing the overall image of a tourist destination. Benchmarking of customer satisfaction in small hospitality businesses results in a drive for innovation with the corresponding effects on a destination's attractiveness (Kozak and Rimmington, 1998).

In the following sections, the basic ideas and guiding principles of the guest satisfaction barometer are described before its methodology is presented. Next, some empirical findings are reported to demonstrate how benchmarks can be used to improve quality and satisfaction. In the final section, we discuss our experience and try to outline some recommendations for future initiatives.

THE GUEST SATISFACTION BAROMETER

In the last years, in several countries, national customer satisfaction indices have been established. The most important ones are the Swedish Customer Satisfaction Barometer, established in 1989 (Fornell, 1992); the "Deutsches Kundenbarometer" in Germany, since 1992 (Meyer and Dornach, 1996); and the "American Index of Customer Satisfaction" (ACSI, since 1994; Fornell et al., 1996). The main reasons for the introduction of such initiatives rely in the importance of quality and satisfaction as key success factors. National customer satisfaction indices deliver valuable information for decision-making at several levels (Eklöf and Westlund, 1998). At a macro–level, they monitor welfare and competitiveness of industries and facilitate appropriate policy formulation. At a company level, they deliver important information on the customer's perceived quality of products and services and allow benchmarking. This information can be the basis for quality strategies and initiatives within the firm. At the consumer level, finally, customer satisfaction indices lead to an increase of welfare as they create quality awareness and competition.

The successful experience with customer satisfaction indices in various countries have inspired the introduction of a customer satisfaction barometer focused on tourism in Austria. Its basic ideas and principles are described below.

Basic Ideas and Guiding Principles

The awareness of the economic consequences of quality and satisfaction, and the idea that each hotel in Austria should monitor quality and satisfaction systematically and regularly were the main driving forces behind the Austrian Guest Satisfaction Barometer. In winter 1999, the "Tirolwerbung" (Tyrolean Tourist Board) and the IFK[1] decided to develop and introduce a method, which allows a systematic measurement and management of customer satisfaction.

It should enable a large number of participating hotels at low costs to

- measure customer satisfaction systematically, regularly, and reliably;
- give clear recommendations for the management of customer satisfaction;
- identify strengths and weaknesses and give indications for improvements; and
- compare their customer's satisfaction ratings with those of competitors.

Some guiding principles have been formulated with regard to these goals as well as previous experiences in several countries with customer satisfaction barometers (e.g., Bruhn and Grund, 2000; Anderson and Fornell, 2000; Eklöf and Westlund, 1998). First, results must be available immediately in order to stimulate effective improvement activities. Second, competitive benchmarking and best-in-class benchmarking must be considered as constitutive characteristics of a customer satisfaction index (Bruhn & Grund, 2000). Third, it has been emphasized by Bruhn and Murmann (1998) that data should be collected by a neutral institution in order to ensure objectivity and acceptance of the results.

Timeliness of Results

Based on an exploratory study with hotel managers interested in participating in the guest satisfaction barometer, it became clear that timeliness of results is one of they key success factors. In order to react quickly to quality problems, it is crucial that results of customer satisfaction surveys are available within the shortest time intervals possible. Only then, can accurate measures be taken. Especially in tourism, where hotels often have a high employee turnover, results have to be available immediately. If they are not available before the end of the season, they often cannot be used for employee evaluation, training purposes, etc. Therefore, each participating hotel gets key results of the survey every three weeks and a comprehensive report at the end of the season. As a consequence, effects of improvement programs can be assessed immediately.

Benchmarking

Information on competitors and the industry as a whole are the key ingredients to each customer satisfaction management program. Therefore, a customer satisfaction barometer should facilitate benchmarking. Each participating hotel gets a comprehensive report with information on the average performance of the industry on each variable that was measured. Although the main principle of benchmarking is to find best-practices (see next paragraph) we decided also to include the average performance of the industry for two reasons. First, for many participating hotels, best-in-class benchmarks are far above what can be reached in the short term. Therefore, the comparison with the average performance gives additional information about their relative competitive position and might be far more motivating. Second, hotels that are among the best-in-class competitors are interested to know to what extend they are above the average or, in other words, what their competitive advantage is. This way, an identification of strengths and weaknesses relative to competitors is possible.

Best-in-Class Orientation and Leading Practices

Quality initiatives and satisfaction programs should be oriented towards quality leadership. Therefore, detailed information on best-in-class competitors is helpful in determining its own position relative to leading competitors. Each participating hotel is compared to the "top box," consisting of the top 25 percent of leading hotels in terms of customer satisfaction. This should stimulate firms to strive for excellence and motivate participating hotels to learn from leading practices.

Data Collection and Analysis by a Neutral Institution

Customer satisfaction measurement programs, if carried out by the firm's own staff, often suffer from a lack of the necessary resources and time constraints. If data is collected and analyzed by a neutral and experienced institution, these tasks can be carried out highly professionally and objectively. Furthermore, costs are expected to be much lower due to experience curve effects and economies of scale. The requirement, that neutral institutions are engaged with data collection and analysis for customer satisfaction barometers in order to ensure objectivity, professionalism, and efficiency, have been stressed by several authors (e.g., Bruhn & Grund, 2000; Bruhn & Murmann, 1998). Finally, competitive information is only obtainable when customer satisfaction ratings of all participating companies are pooled. This can best be done by a third party. However, participating hotels could be reluctant to make confidential information accessible if data is not processed by a neutral institution that guarantees confidentiality.

Methodology

Questionnaire

The guest satisfaction barometer is based on a standardized self-administered questionnaire. It is designed to measure satisfaction with several service attributes including attribute importance, overall satisfaction, price satisfaction, fulfillment of expectations, loyalty, word-of-mouth, and complaining behavior. These variables are measured on 5-point-rating-scales. Open-response questions are included to gather specific incidents that drive satisfaction or dissatisfaction. Furthermore, information on booking behavior and demographics are collected. Table 1 gives an overview on the most important aspects covered in the questionnaire.

TABLE 1. Structure and Content of the Questionnaire

Attribute Satisfaction	Booking:	2 items
	Arrival:	2 items
	Reception:	3 items
	Room:	5 items
	Breakfast:	4 items
	Restaurant:	6 items
	Leisure time facilities:	2 items
	Leisure time program:	2 items
Satisfaction incidents	Positive and negative incidents concerning each attribute	
Attribute importance	For each attribute	
Overall Satisfaction	1 question	
Price Satisfaction	1 question	
Fulfillment of expectations	1 question	
Loyalty	Repurchase intention Word-of-Mouth	
Complaining behavior	Reasons for the complaints Complaining rate Satisfaction with reaction to complaints	
Booking behavior	2 questions	
Demographics	5 questions	

Data Collection

A specified number of questionnaires are left in hotel rooms. In order to ensure high visibility, it is either placed on the bed or on the table. The guest fills out the questionnaire anonymously, puts it into an envelope and leaves it in the hotel room or returns it at the front desk. Anonymity is guaranteed to ensure that guests state their satisfaction truly, and briefly describe incidents that caused satisfaction or dissatisfaction. We consider this as important, as most of these incidents will be related to experiences with employees. Guests could be reluctant to describe these incidents if they have to put their name on the questionnaire. The questionnaires are then collected at the front desk and sent to IFK for data analysis. A minimum of 200 questionnaires should be collected per hotel each year.

Results

Data processing is done continuously and key results are sent to the participating hotels every three weeks. At the end of the season, a detailed report with benchmark information and improvement opportunities is compiled. It contains two sections.

- Firm-specific results (attribute satisfaction and importance, positive and negative incidents, overall satisfaction, price satisfaction, fulfillment of expectations, complaining behavior, repurchase and recommendation intentions, booking behavior, and demographics) and
- Benchmarks (attribute satisfaction, overall satisfaction, price satisfaction, fulfillment of expectations, complaining behavior, repurchase and recommendation intentions, customer value analysis, and importance-performance-analysis).

The reports are structured according to the sequence of the questions in the questionnaire. They include easily comprehensible graphical visualizations and verbal interpretations.

In the following section, we report some empirical findings in order to demonstrate how data from this guest satisfaction barometer can be used to identify strengths and weaknesses, improvement opportunities, benchmarking, and strategic decision-making.

GUEST SATISFACTION BAROMETER AND BENCHMARKING

By the end of 2000, 37 hotels participated in the pilot study. Approximately 3,500 questionnaires were collected. In order to create meaningful benchmarks, hotels are grouped into homogeneous clusters. Most of the participating hotels were members of a special interest group. They cooperate in different areas (marketing, quality management, controlling, etc.) on a regional level. It is their goal to increase their competitiveness by exchanging experience and knowledge. In that case these interest groups formed natural clusters of similar hotels. If a hotel is not a member of such an interest group it is decided individually into which cluster it is integrated. In the following sections, we refer to 13 hotels of such a cluster. These hotels have been successfully working together for a number of years and are committed to the highest quality standards. In the first three months of the pilot study 1,105 questionnaires were collected. The number of questionnaires averaged 85 for each hotel.

Firm-Specific Results

Firm-specific results contain data about satisfaction and dissatisfaction with the measured quality attributes, satisfaction incidents, guest loyalty, complaining and booking behavior, and demographics. These data are delivered on a continuous basis, ideally every three weeks, provided that at least 30 questionnaires have been collected within this time period. These results should enable participating hotels to get a quick customer feedback and therefore to react to quality problems on the spot.

Standardized questions typically reveal the level of satisfaction or dissatisfaction with certain quality attributes. This data is descriptive. In other words, they measure how satisfied or dissatisfied customers are, but do not detect the causes behind a certain satisfaction judgment. Consequently, the specific incidents that are behind the guest's feeling of satisfaction or dissatisfaction are of particular interest. They describe in the guest's own words what the specific reasons were for good or bad service experiences. As such, they contain a clear picture of satisfaction and dissatisfaction drivers and typically provide the starting point for exact short-term improvement activities. Figure 1 shows a customer satisfaction profile of a participating hotel with positive and negative incidents. Satisfaction ratings are converted into percentages. The positive and negative incidents give clear insights into the causes of satisfaction and dissatisfaction. Improvements can easily be derived.

The report with firm-specific results allows for (1) a short-term management of customer satisfaction and (2) a continuous evaluation of the effects of improvement programs.

FIGURE 1. Satisfaction with Hotel-Room

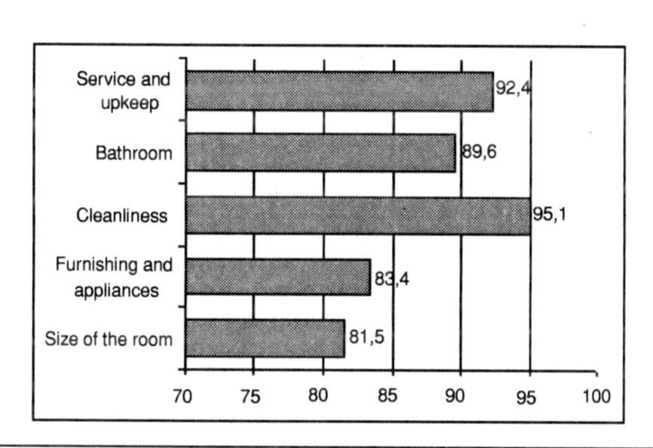

Positive incidents	Negative incidents
• Friendliness of personnel	• Bad ventilation of the bathroom (2x)
• Flexibility of personnel	• Cleaning lady comes too early (3x)
• Two wash-basins (2x)	• Room too small for crib (room 308)
• Cleanliness of Bathroom (2x)	• No possibility/line to dry swimsuits (2x)
•	• Cobwebs on the ceiling (room 207)
	• ..

Benchmarking

Benchmarking information is contained in the comprehensive report at the end of the season. In addition to its own results, each participating hotel receives competition-related results. Clusters of similar hotels are built (e.g., size, location, and market segments), which form the basis for benchmarking. Benchmarking, then, is done on two levels.

First, the average satisfaction scores for these clusters, including loyalty indicators (repurchase intentions and word-of-mouth) and various pieces of information on complaining behavior are provided. Second, the leading 25 percent of hotels concerning customer satisfaction are identified and form the basis for "best-in-class benchmarking."

The following analyses contained in the comprehensive report at the end of the season deliver valuable benchmark opportunities.

- Satisfaction profiles,
- guest loyalty,
- complaining behavior and complaint handling,
- customer value analysis, and
- importance-performance-analysis.

Satisfaction Profiles

Figure 2 contains a customer satisfaction profile of a hotel with benchmark information (percentages). It clearly shows strengths and weaknesses from the customer's point of view compared to competitors in the same cluster.

Whereas satisfaction profiles visualize satisfaction ratings and show the degree of guest satisfaction, the single positive and negative incidents (see Figure 1) deliver the reasons for satisfaction and dissatisfaction. Priorities for improvement activities can be derived from an importance-performance-analysis (see Figure 7).

Loyalty

Repeat purchase and positive word-of-mouth are two main outcomes of customer satisfaction and drivers of profitability. Therefore, they should be measured continuously.

Figure 3 shows the relationship between overall satisfaction and repurchase intentions. Data stems from one of the regional special interest groups described above, consisting of 13 hotels (N = 1,105). The Pearson correlation coefficient for the relationship between overall satisfaction and repurchase

FIGURE 2. Customer Satisfaction Profile with Benchmarks (hotel room)

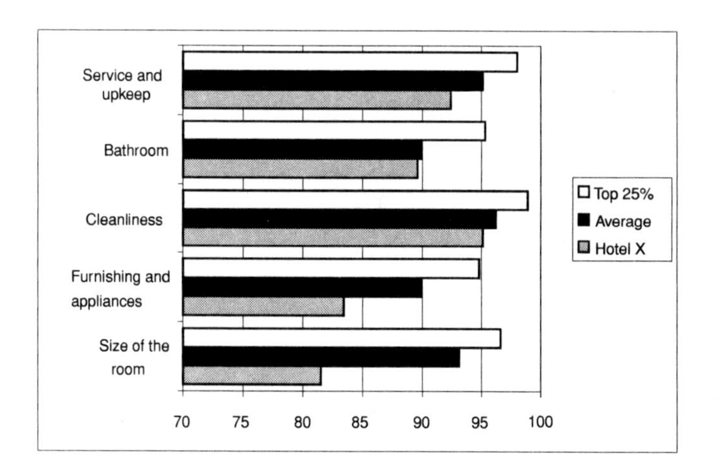

intentions is r = .447, two-tailed significant at .01, and r = .580, two-tailed significant at .01 for the relationship between overall satisfaction and recommendation to others.

It can be seen clearly that very high levels of customer satisfaction have to be achieved (above 80%) in order to increase customer loyalty.

Comparison with average scores of the cluster provides insights into the satisfaction-loyalty relationship (Figure 4). Again, this data stems from the regional special interest group described above. These hotels are committed to the highest quality standards and have outstanding satisfaction ratings. Nevertheless, clear differences can be observed.

Repurchase intentions and the number of guests who recommend the hotel to friends seem to be satisfying for hotel X. They both are on a very high level. Twenty-seven percent of the guests state that they are sure to visit this hotel again and 69% say that they will recommend it to others. However, compared to the average and the top 25% of the hotels in this cluster, the numbers are rather low. Efforts to increase loyalty should be undertaken.

Complaining Behavior

Customer satisfaction is directly related to the number of customer complaints. On the one hand, a higher satisfaction can reduce the number of complaints as quality increases. On the other hand, due to a higher customer orientation, the number of complaints might correlate positively with cus-

FIGURE 3. Satisfaction and Repurchase Intentions, and Recommendation to Others

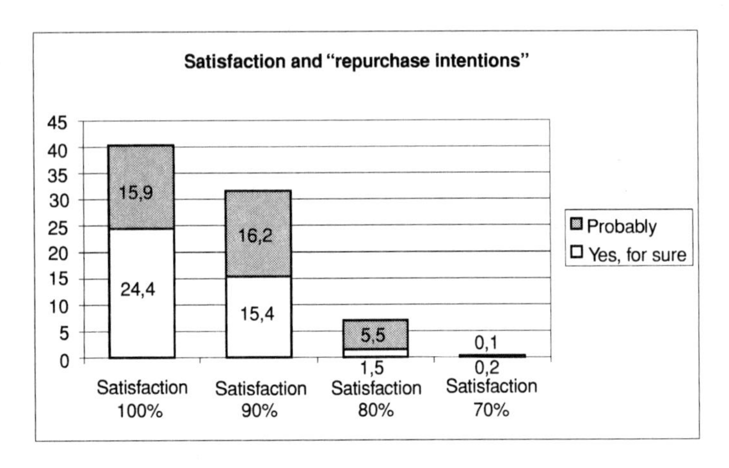

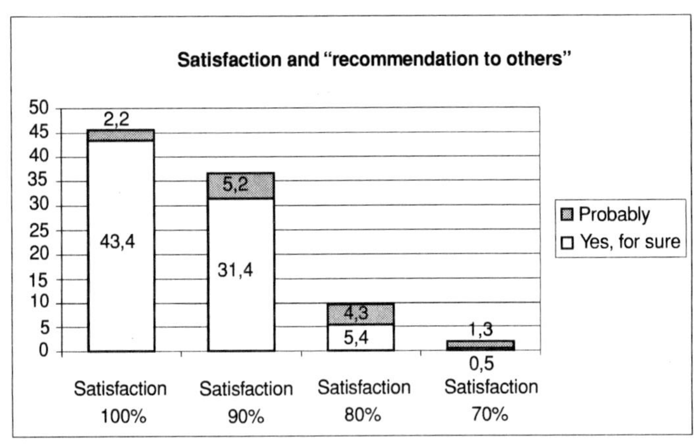

tomer satisfaction. This can be attributed to the fact that satisfaction alone is not the only antecedent of complaining. Dissatisfied customers are reluctant to complain for a number of reasons (e.g., Oliver, 1997). First, the perceived costs (time, effort, etc.) are too high in relation to expected benefits and the probability of success. Second, customers might not have the necessary abilities (knowledge of channels, access to channels, etc.) or motivation (e.g., cultural norms, threat of intimidation, etc.). As a consequence, the number of complaints is no reliable indicator of satisfaction. Therefore, it should be interesting to know what the complaining ratio compared to the competitors is. Fur-

FIGURE 4. Benchmarks on Customer Loyalty

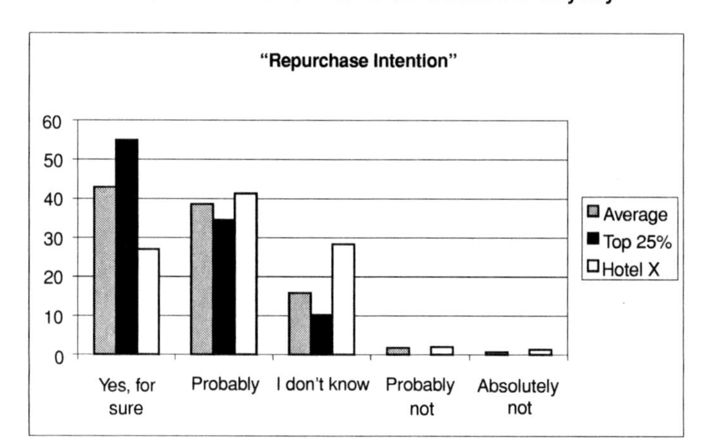

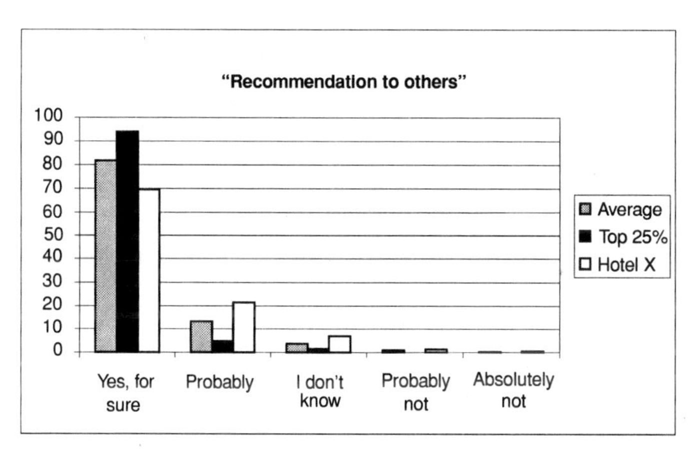

thermore, complaint handling has been identified as a critical determinant of overall satisfaction. A number of empirical studies found that customers whose complaints were positively addressed have a higher percentage of positive word-of-mouth and repurchase intentions than customers who did not complain (Oliver, 1997).

Table 2 gives an overview on complaining behavior in the hotel cluster analyzed. The results are highly interesting. Thirteen percent of the guests experienced a problem. From these, more than 30 percent did not complain. Guests who complain tend to be more loyal. The numbers stress the importance of complaint handling. Guests who are satisfied with service recovery will engage in positive word-of-mouth (77 percent) and are willing to come again (81

TABLE 2. Complaining Behavior

Guest ...	Percentage of guests	Recommend to others, %	Will come again, %
No problem experienced	87	90	91
Problem, did not complain	31	35	23
Problem, complained	69	65	77
Complained, satisfied with recovery	77	77	81
Complained, dissatisfied with recovery	33	14	10
Complained, satisfied with friendliness	89	93	91
Complained, dissatisfied with friendliness	11	4	6

percent). Even more important than redress seems to be the friendliness of employees when customers complain. If complainants are satisfied with friendliness, their likelihood of recommendation and repurchase is even higher than of those guests who experienced no problems.

For these reasons, the following information on complaining behavior is included in the barometer.

- Complaining rates of dissatisfied customers,
- causes of complaints, and
- satisfaction with complaint handling (recovery and friendliness).

Hotel X in Figure 5 seems to have an excellent complaint handling system. Almost 90 percent of dissatisfied guests complain. This is clearly above average. Surprisingly, the complaining rate of guests who experienced a problem in the top 25% hotels is relatively low. One might expect a higher complaining rate in the leading hotels, as they should have established a well working complaint-handling system. One possible explanation for these unexpected results might be related to the causes of problems, which could be minor problems compared to hotels with lower satisfaction ratings. Therefore, guests might be reluctant to complain. In Hotel X satisfaction with recovery is above average, but below the top 25%. The same is true for satisfaction with friendliness of employees during complaint handling. In summary, whereas the complaint-handling system motivates dissatisfied guests to communicate their problems, satisfaction with recovery and friendliness–although already on a high level–can still be improved compared to the leading hotels.

Customer Value Analysis

Customer Value Management has become a key issue in the last years (Woodruff, 1997; Slater, 1997). The idea has also entered research into tour-

FIGURE 5. Complaint Benchmarks

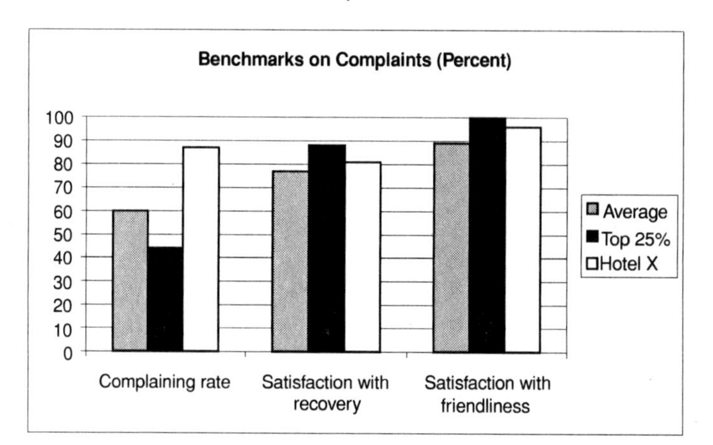

ism and destination management (Kashyap and Bojanic, 2000; Murphy and Pritchard, 1997), giving new meaning and direction to the discussion of quality and customer satisfaction as success factors. The goal is no longer maximum quality and satisfaction. What should be aimed at is a perceived customer value, which is better than that of rival offers. Zeithaml (1988, p. 14) defines customer value as "the consumer's overall assessment of the utility of a product based on perceptions of what is received and what is given."

In the guest satisfaction barometer, these two dimensions are measured using the items "satisfaction with price" and "overall satisfaction with service."

Although price satisfaction and overall satisfaction with service are correlated (Pearson's r = .649, two-sided significant at .01), in many cases guests are satisfied with quality but not with price and vice versa. Therefore, it makes sense to consider these variables separately. This is done using a two-dimensional matrix. "Relative price satisfaction" and "relative service satisfaction" (overall satisfaction with service attributes) are calculated by dividing a hotel's own rating by the average rating in the cluster. Perceived customer value is then represented by a two-dimensional matrix (see Figure 6).

Hotels can be positioned into four quadrants with specific recommendations for the management of customer value.

- *Quadrant I.* Low relative price satisfaction/low relative service satisfaction. They offer poor quality at a high price and, as a consequence, deliver inferior customer value. Companies in this quadrant will have serious problems in the long run and must react quickly.

- *Quadrant II.* High relative price satisfaction/low relative service satisfaction. Here, price seems to be all right, but quality of service is relatively low. These companies are in continuous danger to lose customers, as they are only attracted by the low price. Customers, disappointed with low quality, will not repurchase and might engage in negative word of-mouth.
- *Quadrant III.* Low relative price satisfaction/high relative service satisfaction. These companies have outstanding quality, but the price is too high. Customers are not willing to pay that high price for superior quality. In order to attract and keep guests, these hotels need to increase price satisfaction.
- *Quadrant IV.* High price satisfaction/high relative service satisfaction. Hotels in this quadrant create superior customer value. They can be labeled as "winners."

The positions in these quadrants give a clear picture of the competition. These managerial recommendations form the basis for the formulation of strategies to deliver superior customer value.

FIGURE 6. Customer Value Analysis

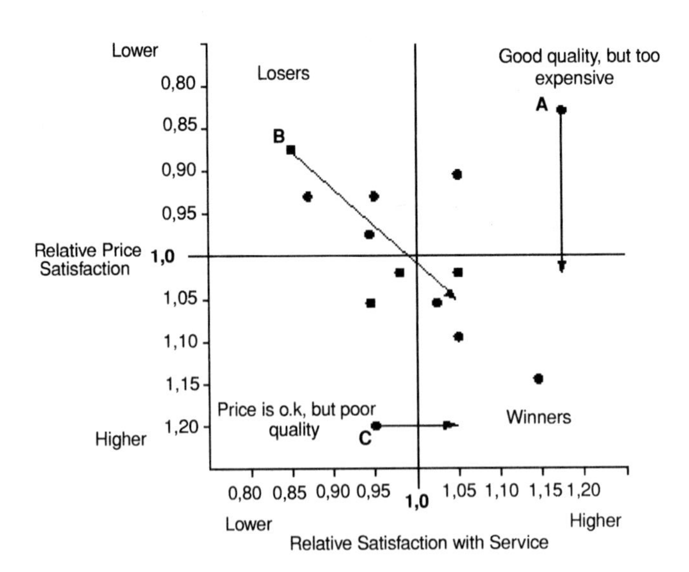

Importance-Performance-Analysis (IPA)

Whereas customer value analysis allows for the formulation of strategies, importance-performance-analysis (IPA) delivers information on how these strategies can be realized. IPA was introduced by Martilla and James (1977) to yield insights into which product or service attributes a company should devote more attention to, and which of them may be consuming too many resources. IPA identifies those attributes that (a) are most important to the customer and have the highest impact on customer satisfaction and (b) have a low performance and need to be improved (see also Weber, 2000). Slack (1994) proposes to take service performance and competitor performance as a composite measure. Using a two-dimensional matrix, where attribute satisfaction relative competitors are depicted along the *y*-axis and importance along the *x*-axes, four specific recommendations for customer satisfaction management can be derived (Figure 7).

A variety of methods exist to measure attribute importance. In their study, Griffin and Hauser (1993) compared three different measures of importance (direct rating, constant-sum scale, and anchored scale) and found no significant differences between the methods. In this project we use a 5-point-rating scale, as it is very easy to use.

Attributes in Quadrant I, evaluated high both in relative satisfaction and importance, represent opportunities for gaining or maintaining competitive advantages. In this area, a hotel should "keep up the good work." Low relative satisfaction on highly important attributes calls for immediate attention (Quadrant II). In order to enhance overall satisfaction, a hotel should concentrate on these attributes. If they are ignored, this poses a serious threat. Quadrant III contains attributes both low in satisfaction and importance. Typically, it is not necessary to focus additional effort here. These service attributes are of "low priority." Attributes located in Quadrant IV are rated high in satisfaction, but low in importance. This implies that resources committed to these attributes would be better employed elsewhere. High performance on unimportant attributes indicates a "possible overkill."

In the guest satisfaction barometer "relative satisfaction" (measured on a 5-point scale: 5 = very satisfied, 1 = very dissatisfied) of an attribute is calculated by subtracting the competitor's attribute satisfaction rating from the satisfaction rating. Attribute performance is measured using a 5-point scale (5 = very important, 1 = not at all important). The mean of the importance ratings are used to divide the matrix into quadrants (Martilla and James, 1977).

In analyzing the Importance-Performance matrix (Figure 7), it can be derived that attributes in Quadrant I are key drivers of customer satisfaction, and the management's job is to ensure that the hotel "keeps up the good work."

FIGURE 7. Importance-Performance-Analysis

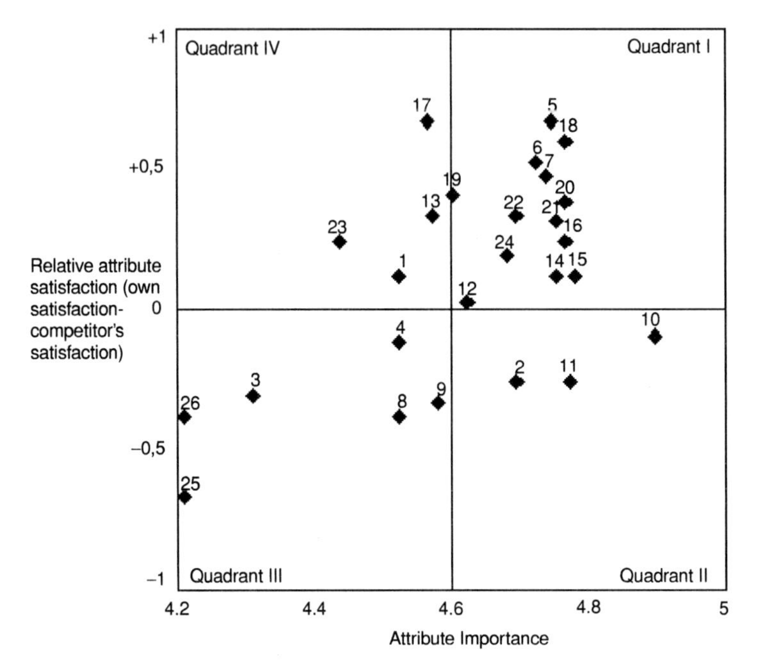

1. Rapidity and competence of reservation
2. Friendliness during reservation
3. Easiness to find hotel
4. First impression of hotel
5. Friendliness at reception
6. Helpfulness at reception
7. Competence at reception
8. Size of room
9. Furnishing and appliances
10. Cleanliness of room
11. Bathroom
12. Room service and keep up
13. Atmosphere in the breakfast room
14. Quality of breakfast
15. Friendliness of employees at breakfast
16. Overall breakfast service
17. Atmosphere in the restaurant
18. Quality of food
19. Quality of drinks
20. Friendliness of waiters
21. Overall service in restaurant
22. Price-quality-ratio in restaurant
23. Leisure time infrastructure
24. Cleanliness of leisure time infrastructure
25. Information about leisure time programme
26. Entertainment value of leisure time programme

"Leisure time infrastructures" can be viewed as areas of performance "overkill." They are relatively unimportant to the customers, but the hotel performs very well. Management might wish to reallocate resources to high-priority areas. Cleanliness of room and bathrooms, as well as friendliness during reservations, are areas that need improvement because satisfaction is low and importance is high. "Information about leisure time programs" and their "entertainment value" are attributes of low priority in this case. Their poor performance is apparently not a problem, as they are relatively unimportant.

IPA is a valuable tool in defining improvement priorities. Positive and negative incidents, as depicted in Figure 1, give detailed hints on how poor quality can be improved. In a relatively high number of cases, cobwebs on the ceiling, bad ventilation in the bathroom, and no opportunities or lines to dry swimsuits in the bathroom were in part responsible for the low satisfaction with the cleanliness of the room and the bathroom in general. These problems should easily be solvable.

Conclusions and Recommendations

Customer satisfaction is of utmost importance as it is directly related to profitability. Therefore, it needs to be measured systematically and regularly. This, however, is rarely done in practice. Furthermore, most customer satisfaction management tools require some form of competitor information that typically is not available. A guest satisfaction barometer, as it is presented in this paper, seems to be a promising approach. It enables a large number of participating hotels to measure customer satisfaction systematically, regularly, and reliably at low costs. Results give clear recommendations for the management of customer satisfaction, they help to identify strengths and weaknesses and give indications for improvements. Finally, it is possible to compare customer's satisfaction ratings with those of competitors.

According to our experience, the following requirements should be fulfilled in order to benefit from such an initiative.

1. A high number of participating hotels.

Benchmarking is one of the guiding principles of the guest satisfaction barometer. To be able to create meaningful benchmarks, a large number of hotels have to be included in the project. If this is the case, homogeneous clusters can be built and competitor information is highly relevant. In the pilot study we used the top 25 percent to define the best-practicing companies. This however, this sample proved to be too low. A large number of hotels were very close to this benchmark. For this reason it was decided to reduce the best-in-class benchmark to the top 10 percent companies in each cluster.

2. Low costs for the participating hotels.

The Alpine hotel sector is characterized by highly fragmented business structures. Micklewright (1993) states that small businesses that lack the resources and inclination to carry out benchmarking are the ones that could most benefit from it. Costs (monetary costs, time, and resources) for the hotels should be kept at a minimum. This also enables relatively small hotels to participate in and to take advantage of the barometer's benefits.

3. Data collection and analysis by a neutral institution.

If data is collected and analyzed by an experienced and neutral institution, these tasks are carried out professionally and objectively. Due to experience curve effects and economies of scale, such a barometer is very cost efficient.

4. Standardized questionnaire combined with open-response questions.

In order to obtain comparable data, it is necessary to standardize the questionnaire to a high extent. On the other hand, drivers of satisfaction and dissatisfaction should be identified. This can be done by open-response questions collecting data on positive and negative incidents. These incidents typically give valuable insights into what is behind certain satisfaction ratings.

5. Fast availability of results.

This is a key success factor. Participating hotels need customer feedback as soon as possible. One final report at the end of the season would not do it. Therefore, the most important results should be provided in short time intervals. This requires continuous data collection and analysis.

In summary, the positive experience from the pilot phase was the deciding factor to continue the project and to increase the number participating hotels. In the year 2001, it is planned to include at least 100 hotels and to collect on average 200 questionnaires per hotel.

NOTE

1. Institut für Kundenzufriedenheit (Institute for Customer Satisfaction), a market research and consulting company in Innsbruck/Austria.

REFERENCES

Anderson, E. W. & Fornell, C. (2000). Foundations of the American Customer Satisfaction Index. In: *Total Quality Management*, Vol. 11, No. 7, 869-882.

Anderson, E. W., Fornell, C. & Lehmann, D. R. (1994). Customer Satisfaction, Market Share and Profitability: Findings from Sweden. *Journal of Marketing*, 58 (July), 53-66.

Anderson, E. W. & Fornell, C. (2000). Foundations of the American Customer Satisfaction Index. In: *Total Quality Management*, 11, 7, 869-882.

Bruhn, M. & Grund M, A. (2000). Theory, Development and Implementation of National Customer Satisfaction Indices: The Swiss Index of Customer Satisfaction (SWICS). *Total Quality Management*, 11, 7, 1017-1028.

Bruhn, M. & Murmann, B. (1998). *Nationale Kundenbarometer. Messung von Qualität und Zufriedenheit. Methodenvergleich und Entwurf eines Schweizer Kundenbarometers*. Wiesbaden: Gabler Verlag.

Eklöf, J. A. & Westlund, A. (1998). Customer Satisfaction Index and its Role in Quality Management *Total Quality Management*, Vol. 9 (4&5), 80-85.

Fornell, C. (1992). A National Customer Satisfaction Barometer. The Swedish Experience. *Journal of Marketing*, 56, 6-21.

Fornell, C., Johnson, M. D., Anderson, E. W. Cha, J. & Bryant, B. E. (1996). The American Customer Satisfaction Index. Nature, Purpose and Findings. *Journal of Marketing*, 60, 7-18.

Griffin, A. and J.R. Hauser (1993). The Voice of the Customer. *Marketing Science*, 12, 1, pp. 1-27.

Kashyap R., Bojanic D. C. (2000). A Structural Analysis of Value, Quality, and Price Perceptions of Business and Leisure Travelers. *Journal of Travel Research*, 39, (1), 45-51.

Kozak, M. and Rimmington, M. (1998). Benchmarking: Destination Attractiveness and Small Hospitality Business Performance. *International Journal of Contemporary Hospitality Management*, 10(5), 184-188.

Martilla, J. A. and James J. C. (1977). Importance-Performance Analysis. *Journal of Marketing*, 41, 77-79.

Meyer, A. & Dornach, F. (1996). *Das Deutsche Kundenbarometer 1996–Qualität und Zufriedenheit–Jahrbuch der Kundenzufriedenheit in Deutschland 1996*. Munich: Deutsche Marketing-Vereinigung e.V. and Deutsche Post AG.

Micklewright, M.J. (1993). Competitive benchmarking: large gains for small companies. *Quality Progress*, June, 67-68.

Murphy P. E., Pritchard, M. (1997). Destination Price-Value Perceptions: An Examination of Origin and Seasonal Influences. *Journal of Travel Research*, 35, (3), 16-23.

Oliver, R. L. (1997). *Customer Satisfaction. A Behavioral Perspective on the Consumer*. New York et al.: Mc Graw-Hill

Reichheld, F. F. & Sasser, W. E. (1990). Zero Defections: Quality Comes to Services. *Harvard Business Review*, 68 (September-October), 105-111.

Slack, N. (1994), The Importance-Performance Matrix as a Determinant of Improvement Priority. *International Journal of Operations & Production Management*, 14, 5, 59-75.

Slater, St. F. (1997). Developing a Customer Value-Based Theory of the Firm. *Journal of the Academy of Marketing Science*, 25, (2), 164-130.

Weber, K. (2000). Meeting Planners' Perceptions of Hotel-chain Practices and Benefits. *Cornell Hotel and Restaurant Administration Quarterly*, August, 32-38.

Woodruff, R. B. (1997). Customer Value: The Next Source for Competitive Advantage. *Journal of the Academy of Marketing Science*, 25, (2), 139-153.

Zeithaml, V. A. (1988). Consumer Perceptions of Price, Quality, and Value: A Means-End Model and Synthesis of Evidence. *Journal of Marketing*, 52, July, 2-22.

Zeithaml, V. A. (2000). Service Quality, Profitability, and the Economic Worth of Customers: What We Know and What We Need to Learn. *Journal of the Academy of Marketing Science*, 58 (1), 67-85.

APPENDIX

ATTRIBUTE SATISFACTION	5-Point-Rating Scale (5=very satisfied, 1=not satisfied at all)
ATTRIBUTE IMPORTANCE	5-Point-Rating Scale (5=very important, 1=not important at all)
Booking	a) Rapidity and competence b) Friendliness
Arrival	a) Easiness to find (signs etc.) b) First impression of the hotel
Reception	a) Friendliness of employees b) Helpfulness of employees c) Competence of employees
Room	a) Size of the room b) Furnishing and appliances c) Cleanliness d) Bathroom e) Service and upkeep
Breakfast	a) Atmosphere in the breakfast room b) Quality of breakfast c) Friendliness of Employees d) Overall service
Restaurant	a) Atmosphere in the restaurant b) Food c) Drinks d) Friendliness of employees e) Overall service f) Value for money
Leisure Time Facilities	a) Offer b) Cleanliness
Leisure Time Program	a) Information about the programme b) Adventure/entertainment value
POSITIVE AND NEGATIVE INCIDENTS (for each area)	a) What was positive? (open-response question) b) What was negative? (open-response question)
OVERALL SATISFACTION	0% = completely dissatisfied, 100% = completely satisfied
FULFILLMENT OF EXPECTATIONS	5 = Much better than expected, 1 = Much worse than expected
PRICE SATISFACTION	0% = completely dissatisfied, 100% = completely satisfied
REPURCHASE INTENTION	5 = Yes, for sure, 1 = no, definitely not

RECOMMENDATION TO OTHERS	5 = Yes, for sure, 1 = no, definitely not
COMPLAINING BEHAVIOR	a) Reason to complain (yes, no) b) What was the reason? (open-response question) c) Did guest complain (yes, no) d) To whom? (open-response question)
SATISFACTION WITH REACTION TO COMPLAINT	a) Rapidity and professional behaviour b) Kindness(5-Point-Rating Scale (5=very satisfied, 1=not satisfied at all)
GENERAL INFORMATION	a) Main reason of stay b) Traveling with .... c) Booking behavior d) Age e) Gender f) Country of Origin

A Heuristic Model for Benchmarking SME Hotel and Restaurant Businesses on the Internet

Karl W. Wöber

SUMMARY. In this paper, the author introduces a heuristic procedure for the identification of benchmarking partners in an interactive database environment. The purpose of this paper is to present the applicability of the procedure for benchmarking hotel and restaurant operations on the Internet. The decision support system which is used for this experimental study is accessible on the World Wide Web where the data is obtained from Austrian small and medium-sized hotel enterprises. The system is based on a weighting model which uses managerial judgements in order to identify similar hotel and restaurant businesses and to guarantee representative samples for the analysis. It enables Austrian entrepreneurs as well as consultancy companies specializing in tourism to compare the performance of hotel and restaurant enterprises with others of a similar nature. In the present paper, the author gives a comprehensive description of the conceptual approach, the technical realization and experiences and implications with the system. *[Article copies available for a fee from The Haworth Document Delivery Service: 1-800-HAWORTH. E-mail address: <getinfo@haworthpressinc.com> Website: <http://www.HaworthPress.com> © 2001 by The Haworth Press, Inc. All rights reserved.]*

Karl W. Wöber is affiliated with the Institute for Tourism and Leisure Studies, Vienna University of Economics and Business Administration, Austria, Augasse 2-6, 1090 Vienna, Austria (E-mail: karl.woeber@wu-wien.ac.at).

[Haworth co-indexing entry note]: "A Heuristic Model for Benchmarking SME Hotel and Restaurant Businesses on the Internet." Wöber, Karl W. Co-published simultaneously in *Journal of Quality Assurance in Hospitality & Tourism* (The Haworth Hospitality Press, an imprint of The Haworth Press, Inc.) Vol. 2, No. 3/4, 2001, pp. 49-70; and: *Benchmarks in Hospitality and Tourism* (ed: Sungsoo Pyo) The Haworth Hospitality Press, an imprint of The Haworth Press, Inc., 2001, pp. 49-70. Single or multiple copies of this article are available for a fee from The Haworth Document Delivery Service [1-800-HAWORTH, 9:00 a.m. - 5:00 p.m. (EST). E-mail address: getinfo@haworthpressinc.com].

KEYWORDS. Hospitality management, SMEs (small and medium enterprises), benchmarking, decision support systems, internet

INTRODUCTION

Benchmarking is a buzzword of the last decade of the twenty-first century. This management approach to identify *who is best?* and *what makes them so successful?* has experienced increased popularity, both by manufacturing and service companies. In management science, benchmarking is usually positioned as being an extension of an existing total quality program, and as being a way in which to establish new, more relevant and efficient standards of performance. The increased interest in benchmarking has certainly been stimulated with the publication of Xerox's manager Robert Camp's book on benchmarking (Camp, 1989). Since then, the phenomenon of benchmarking has been discussed by many authors primarily in the form of management guidebooks (e.g., Spendolini, 1992; Watson, 1992; Zairi, 1996; Cross, 1998).

Benchmarking is about learning how to improve business activity, processes and management. The great success of benchmarking in recent years is probably related to its inherent characteristic of being a knowledge-sharing and motivational process. It encourages managers and their staff to think in terms of performance measures and practices to increase profitability. Motwani et al. (1996) conduct a rigorous review of the literature relating to implementation issues of quality management in the hospitality industry, and show how the basic streams of definition and conceptual models relate to form the current practices of quality management within the industry. They propose a five-stage model for the implementation of quality management, and stress the need for benchmarking within this context. In fact, comparing performance figures is the procedure in the benchmarking processes that seems to be accepted and applied by tourism managers rather than more complex procedures like analysing or optimising.

The majority of benchmarking studies can be found in the accommodation sector. Kozak and Rimmington examine the role of benchmarking within the microstructured hospitality sector (Kozak and Rimmington, 1998). While benchmarking activity is growing in large organisations (e.g., Horwath International, 1998; Pannell Kerr Forster, 1998), there has been limited application among small hospitality businesses (e.g., Bottomley, 1995; Sundgaard et al., 1998). Monkhouse (1995) examines the penetration of the small- to medium-sized enterprise (SME) sector by the rapidly growing practice of benchmarking. Following a survey of over 200 SMEs, which clearly identified a 'performance information gap,' the author has undertaken extensive quantitative and qualitative interviews with 25 senior managers. Findings provide a comprehensive picture of both current usage and the perceived or actual barriers to greater use of benchmarking. Monkhouse concludes that the practice of benchmarking in SMEs is embryonic and that little progress can be made by even enlightened managers until the barriers are understood. She also argues that a range of tools and techniques which are capable of accommodating the idiosyncrasies of small businesses need to be developed and made accessible. Additionally, Kozak and Rimmington (1998) find it significant that the examples of benchmarking carried out among small tourism businesses have almost all been carried out by external third parties, who first benefit from the data before they provide information back to the industry.

Still, there are benefits from tourism-related benchmarking studies. Breiter and Kline (1995) considered the role of benchmarking in hotel quality. Boger et al. (1999) identify and compare different levels of discounting among various lodging companies. The findings should assist managers in benchmarking the current discounting practices in lodging companies.

Based on a comprehensive exploratory study by Phillips (1996a, b), Phillips and Moutinho (1998a, b; 1999) propose a managerial tool, called the 'strategic planning index' (also 'marketing planning index'), which measures the effectiveness of strategic planning (or marketing) activities and should facilitate a company's benchmarking process. The tool was tested in the UK hotel sector by a self-evaluation of 63 hotel managers concerning three dimensions of performance: effectiveness, efficiency and adaptability. Effectiveness was measured by three ratios, namely occupancy percentage, average room rate, and growth in sales per room; efficiency by return on investment and profit margin; adaptability by the number of successful new services/products introduced and the percentage of sales accounting for new services/products. A comprehensive list of strategic planning (or marketing) activities were factor analysed and studied by regression analysis to assess various performance indicators. The results of their study indicate that performance is an important measure of strategic planning and marketing effectiveness and that adaptability has a tremendous impact on the ability to maintain competitive advantages in operating efficiencies. In another paper generated from the same dataset Phillips and Appiah-Adu (1998) focus on the value of benchmarking for the qualitative assessment of business processes. The authors review the concept of benchmarking and argue that the appreciation of a firm's relative position is a vital component of strategic planning.

Min and Min (1996; 1997) chronicle the process by which a competitive benchmarking study of service quality provided by six luxury Korean hotels was carried out. In this study attribute evaluations and weightings were determined by questionnaires completed by both employees and guests. Although the authors generate benchmarking scores for each of the six hotels and provide sensitivity analysis for each of the service attributes, they did not give much emphasis to the selection process for benchmarking partners.

Dubé et al. (1999) conducted the most comprehensive study of the US lodging industry's best practices to date (April 2001). The study, which the authors themselves describe as a mammoth undertaking, was conducted under the umbrella of Cornell University's School of Hotel Administration and was financed by American Express (a focus section can be found in volume 40(5) and additional articles in volume 40(6) of the Cornell Hotel and Restaurant Administration Quarterly which give a summary of the research findings on this project.). The study resulted in a compilation of what the authors and a group of industry practitioners considered to be most effective strategies and techniques used by the lodging industry's best operators. The selection of the best practice champions was based on managerial judgement. First the authors drew nominations for best-practice champions via a survey among 610 industry practitioners by mail, fax, and e-mail, as well as from a Web-site where individuals could download the survey. The survey resulted in 3,528 nominations, including self-nominations which were allowed. Given this information, the authors performed in-depth interviews with a list of 549 pre-screened best-practice champions derived from the nominations received and the preparation of case summaries. From this information, a total of 29 overall best-practice hotels were derived. In subsequent articles, the authors have focused more closely on best practices in marketing (Siguaw and Enz, 1999a), food and beverage management (Siguaw and Enz, 1999b), and hotel operations (Siguaw and Enz, 1999c).

LIMITATIONS OF TRADITIONAL BENCHMARKING EFFORTS

Practically all of the benchmarking efforts in tourism ignore, for the most part, differences in operating environments, service levels, and rely on simple engineering ratios. Further problems arise when simple benchmarking studies classify a data set of company statistics into a limited number of groups and provide means and medians for comparisons. The number and type of groups is mostly driven by expert judgements and is confined by the sample size and coding available in the data. It goes without saying, that to be really useful, benchmarking partners should also match on levels of service provided, difficulty of operating environments, etc. Practices that are efficient and productive in one environment may not be relevant or helpful in a different environment.

In general one sees that more sophisticated initiatives spend more effort on the right selection of benchmarking partners. However, in the studies reviewed one does not find a system that could be easily adapted by other companies. The great majority of these studies are descriptions of counselling projects and do not leave a case-study similar stage. This type of research is of very little value (and sometimes even useless) for other companies who are searching for appropriate benchmarking partners. Therefore, it seems highly desirable that the methods for selecting leadership companies follow an explicit procedure which is valid for a broad range of companies. Furthermore, beyond isolating the most relevant benchmarking partners, there is also the need for methodologies which set up consumption targets and facilitate extensive sensitivity analyses.

Comparing financial information has proved to be effective for the assessment of internal operating performance related to budgeting and past results, whereas common size analysis facilitates operating performance comparisons on an inter-company and industry basis (Harris and Brown, 1998). Each of those methods encompass the idea of a more informed approach to results analysis by the presence of 'absolute' and 'relative' measures of variation in performance. There are basically three ways that management can evaluate and control business performance; these are

1. Comparing budgeted versus actual input and output factors;
2. Comparing input and output factors over multiple periods; and
3. Comparing input and output factors with main competitors.

The first two instruments can be implemented within a firm and without incorporating any external data from other companies. The latter refers to performance monitoring and measurement between 'organizational units.' Organizational units may refer to internal departments, several outlets of one company, or several companies within one industry. For example, by measuring the efficiency of its internal divisions, a company will understand their *relative* performance. This helps the managers to check if any appropriate corrective action needs to be taken and provides indications as to what kind of action, if any, should be taken.

A conceptual model for competitive performance measurement is illustrated in Figure 1. In the discussion to follow, assume that there are N companies to be evaluated. Each company consumes varying components of different discretionary (X^D) and non-discretionary (X^N) inputs to produce different outputs (Y). Non-discretionary factors are uncontrollable to the manager as they are either determined by a company's market area (location of a hotel), or by physical characteristics of the property (number and mix of

FIGURE 1. A Conceptual Model for Competitive Performance Measurement

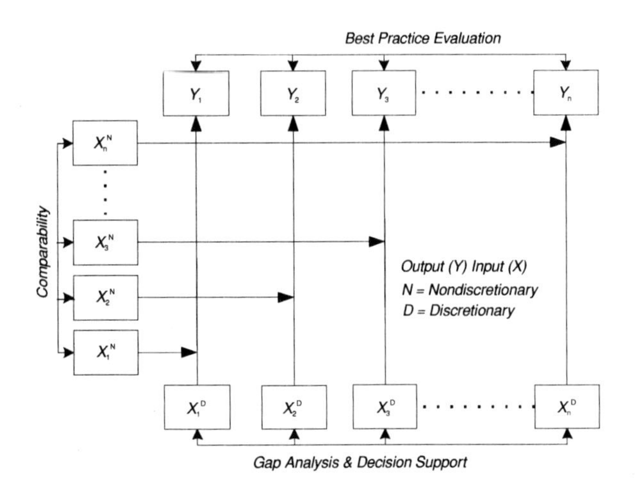

rooms). They are more or less fixed in a sense that they cannot be changed by the management and are commonly interpreted as the environmental constraints in efficiency measurement. Specifically, a company consumes various amounts of discretionary and non-discretionary inputs and produces various amounts of output.

The relationship between the input and output factors leads to the analysis of a production function. Each company may have a different production function depending on the efficiency of the company. Hence, the majority of business performance research initiatives explore the shape of individual production functions and try to find the optimal, or best possible one. For an individual company, detailed information about deviations from the optimal production function could be extremely helpful for management. Unfortunately, the optimal production function is unknown and can only be estimated and tested empirically.

There are several approaches that can be used to estimate a composite production function, either by central tendency, or by frontier analysis. In central tendency techniques, including average ratio analysis (Thanassoulis et al., 1996), regression analysis (Cubbin and Tzanidakis, 1998) or neural networks (Athanassopoulos and Curram, 1996), the best practice surface is given by the best fit curve fitted throughout the data set. In the general case, these methods result in classifications concerning above or below an average efficient firm.

A second possibility is by estimating, or actually calculating, a best practice frontier, which is also called the production frontier. The production frontier represents the maximum output attainable from each input level; hence, it reflects the current state of technology in an industry. Firms in that industry (or represented in a given data set) operate either on that frontier, if they are technically efficient, or beneath the frontier if they are not technically efficient. Frontiers have been estimated using many different methods in efficiency studies. The two principal methods are (1) Data Envelopment Analysis (Morey and Dittman, 1995; Anderson et al. 2000; Wöber, 2000b), and (2) stochastic frontiers (Anderson et al., 1999), which involve mathematical programming and econometric methods, respectively.

Whenever the amount or quality of data is a problem and standard statistical procedures fail, managerial judgements may be used instead. In the following a heuristic procedure for the selection of benchmarking partners is introduced. The system is based on a weighting model which uses managerial judgements in order to identify similar hotel and restaurant businesses and to guarantee representative samples for the analysis.

The multi-dimensional performance measurement system envisaged here requires the gathering and dissemination of large amounts of information across many functions and levels of an organisation. Considering the speed and flexibility of modern information technology systems it is obvious, that this systems can be used to support performance measurement processes (Brignall and Ballantine, 1996:23; Halachmi, 2000). Many authors recognise the continuing importance of technology for the hospitality industry as being a major force in providing competitive advantages especially in the areas of productivity, management decision-making, and education and training (Durocher and Niman, 1993; Go and Pine, 1995; Kluge, 1996; Kirk and Pine, 1998). However, the manner in which information systems are implemented in hotels generally evolves over time, and is rarely planned with executives' decision-making needs in mind. In addition, the information systems used by managers often lag behind the techniques available to them. As a result, although an executive may be deluged with printouts, reports, and statistics, he or she is not necessarily receiving the kinds of information needed to plan and to manage (Geller 1985; Umbreit and Eder, 1987).

The system introduced here uses a heuristic model for the selection of benchmarking partners. The system's functionality is demonstrated with a case-example based on the Austrian Hotel and Restaurant Panel survey. The technical realization is presented and experiences with the system are discussed.

THE AUSTRIAN HOTEL AND RESTAURANT PANEL

In Austria, the development of the Austrian Hotel and Restaurant Panel (AHRP) was an initiative of the Austrian Professional Hotel Association and the Austrian Professional Restaurant Association of the Federal Chamber of Commerce which started in the late 1960s. These associations have realised that Austrian small and medium-sized enterprises cannot cope with a deficiency of comparative financial information on their own. Since 1968, these two organizations have financed an annual survey of Austrian hotel and restaurants that is performed by the Austrian Society for Applied Tourism Research (ASART).

For the AHRP, financial information is collected annually on a confidential basis from between 1,000 and 1,300 hotels and restaurants. The data is collected either from interested companies that voluntarily participated in this project (15.0%), consultancy companies (5.5%), and co-operating industry organizations which are Österreichische Hotel-und Tourismusbank (55.6%) and BÜRGES Förderungsbank des BmwA (23.9%; percentages represent average share of companies provided to the AHRP project by the different parties.). The sample size varies between 2 and 3 percent of all hotels, restaurants and similar accommodation and/or F&B providers in Austria, which is similar to other studies in this field.

The data comprises information from a companies' balance sheet, and the profit and loss statement, and information obtained from an additional questionnaire. The detail of information in the accounting part of the survey follows the most common definitions in the Austrian hotel and restaurant accounting system.

Performance analysis solely based on accounting information does not reflect many aspects of operational productivity and neglects important differences between various forms of businesses. For instance, accounting data usually do not capture information about the number of employees and the distribution of the personal resources in the different cost centres. Especially in the hotel sector, financial reports do not indicate the number of overnights generated during the fiscal year, nor do they give information about the available (maximum) capacities. Hence, even the simple calculation of more valuable ratios of productivity requires additional information on certain business characteristics.

In AHRP, the non-financial data is obtained using an additional questionnaire that is filled out either by the general manager himself or by the tax consultant in charge of the accounting issues. Information captured by questionnaire includes the type of accommodation or food and beverage supply, average annual capacity, number of employees, number of days of operation, number of overnights, the geographical region where the business is located, and the form of ownership. The definition of the variables defined in the AHRP is reported by Wöber (2000a).

The AHRP System's Reporting Features

To foster the increased information needs by Austrian hotel and restaurant entrepreneurs it was decided to disseminate information from the AHRP by the Internet. Therefore, the database generated by the project was integrated into the Tourism Marketing Information System TourMIS (see http://tourmis.wu-wien.ac.at). TourMIS is an Extranet application developed by the Austrian National Tourist Office and the Austrian Society for Applied Research in Tourism with the objective of assisting tourism managers with market research and interactive decision support tools (see Figure 2).

The AHRP site within TourMIS consists of a data entry section and a retrieval section. These are available for active and passive participants alike. It should be noted that the system is accessible to all Austrian hotel and restaurant managers, including those who do not contribute to the survey.

Each entrepreneur who wants to participate at the AHRP and is interested in using the Internet for data entry and reporting has to get an account within TourMIS. TourMIS offers all features of a user database which are necessary when assigning a personal account to each entrepreneur entering the system. These features include an on-line registration of users, an automatic assignment of a password via e-mail, and the editing and deleting of his/her account.

After the entrepreneur's registration he enters his basic business data to the AHRP site and receives a company number which he will need later for editing and in order to perform analyses. User identification, password, and company number offer enough security for the participants. This is necessary to guarantee the level of privacy someone expects when he hands in his financial information to AHRP.

Once the manager has entered his basic business data, which is static information and unlikely to change over the years (e.g., the company's address, location and type of operations), he/she can start entering financial data from the gain and loss statement and the balance sheet as well as the additional business data from the general questionnaire. Consistency checks during the storing phase (e.g., sum checks for the financial information) insure that typing mistakes are avoided and the number of missing values are kept at a minimum. Financial data for multiple consecutive years can be entered into the system.

Data entered by the user may pass all consistency checks during the data entry phase, but still be subject to errors. Although the compulsory identification and the built-in consistency checks support the avoidance of faked entries, this

FIGURE 2. Homepage of Austrian Hotel and Restaurant Panel

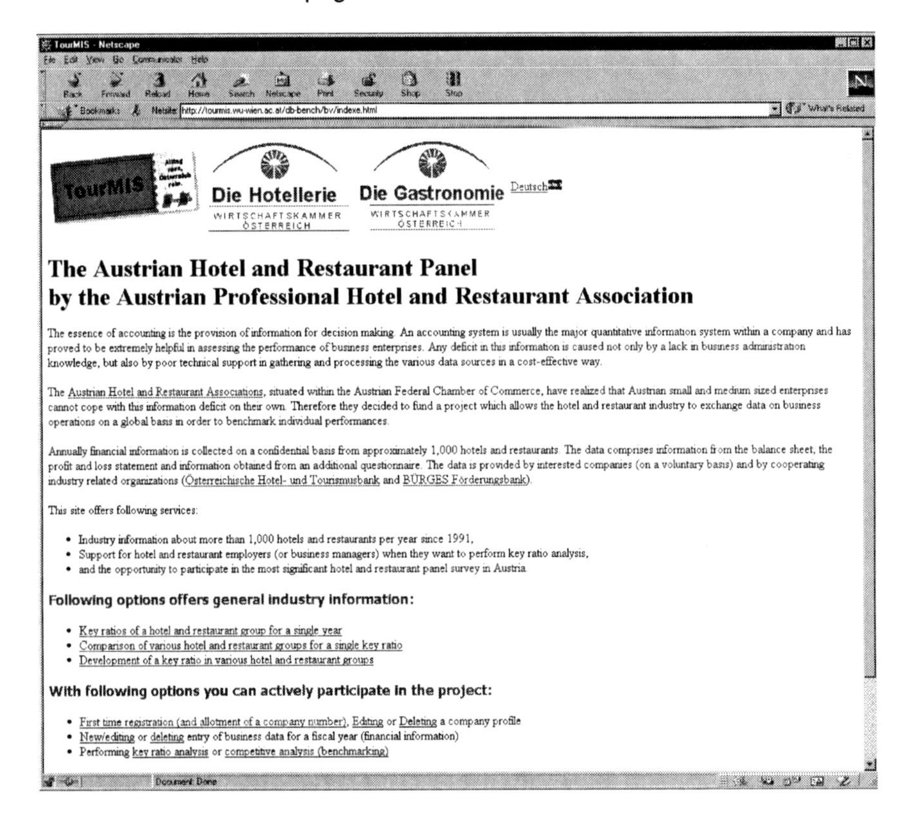

cannot be completely prevented due to the open system architecture. This characteristic of every interactive database application on the Web makes real-time analyses with a pooled data set difficult, as data for analysis may still be corrupt. In order to avoid this problem in the AHRP database the entrepreneur's business data is not directly saved to the general database, it is first saved to a temporary database for all new entries. Periodically the system administrator checks each individual record in the temporary database and decides whether the record is a serious contribution to the project. Records accepted are moved to the general database, and others deleted. Whenever a manager of a company with an unproved data record requires the consideration of several companies for comparative analysis, the analyses are performed on the general database plus exactly one record (the record from the company under evaluation) from the temporary database. This procedure guarantees the integrity of the AHRP database and at the same time allows all conceivable procedures for the optimal selection of comparison partners.

The system's basic retrieval and reporting functions offer the calculation of financial key ratios for each individual company plus the calculation of means, medians, maximum/minimum values, and standard deviations for various strategic groups listed in Table 1. The reporting is organized by pre-formatted tables which are generated on request by means of CGI scripts and an Xbase compatible database. (The program was developed in PERL and uses the Xbase–Perl module written by Pratap Pereira). The principal reports available within AHRP include (1) The calculation of financial key ratios for one specific strategic group/industry sector; (2) The comparison of one specific financial key ratio for all strategic groups/industry sectors; (3) The development of a specific financial key ratio in all strategic groups/industry sectors; (4) The development of all financial key ratios for a specific company over several consecutive fiscal years; and (5) The comparison of an individual company's financial key ratios with a specific strategic group/industry sector.

Reports (1) to (3) are general reports available also to non-participating hotel and restaurant managers or other interested parties accessing the system (see *http://tourmis.wu-wien.ac.at/db-bench/bv/indexe.html*). The tables gener-

TABLE 1. Strategic Groups in the Austrian Hotel and Restaurant Panel

	Hotels or similar accommodation provider		***Restaurants or similar F&B provider***
1	Cat. 5/4, Vienna, annually open	20	Restaurants, category 1, perfect ownership
2	Cat. 5/4, mid-size towns, annually open	21	Restaurants, category 1, rented place
3	Cat. 5/4, small towns, annually open	22	Restaurants, category 2, perfect ownership
4	Cat. 3, Vienna, annually open	23	Restaurants, category 3, rented place
5	Cat. 3, mid-size towns, annually open	24	Inns, cat. 1, perfect ownership, > 10 empl.
6	Cat. 3, small towns, annually open	25	Inns, cat. 1, perfect ownership, ≤ 10 empl.
7	Cat. 1/2, Vienna, annually open	26	Inns, category 1, rented place, > 10 employees
8	Cat. 1/2, mid-size towns, annually open	27	Inns, category 1, rented place, ≤ 10 employees
9	Cat. 1/2, small towns, annually open	28	Inns, category 2, perfect ownership
10	Cat. 5/4, seasonally open: summer and winter	29	Inns, category 2, rented place
11	Cat. 3, seasonally open: summer and winter	30	Coffee-house, category 1, perfect ownership
12	Cat. 1/2, seasonally open: summer and winter	31	Coffee-house, category 1, rented place
13	Spa hotels	32	Coffee-house, category 2, perfect ownership
14	Cat. 5/4, seasonally open: only summer	33	Coffee-house, category 2, rented place
15	Cat. 3, seasonally open: only summer	34	Bars and buffets
16	Cat. 1/2, seasonally open: only summer		
17	Cat. 5/4, seasonally open: only winter		
18	Cat. 3, seasonally open: only winter		
19	Cat. 1/2, seasonally open: only winter		

ated by reports (4) and (5) require active participation by entering individual company data. Tables in (5) provide the simplest form of evaluation which in most hospitality industry reports is referred to as 'benchmarks' of industry performance (e.g., Bottomley, 1995; Pannell Kerr Foster, 1998; Horwath International, 1998).

There are numerous financial ratios that are commonly used by hotel managers to monitor business performance. In the AHRP system, 32 key financial ratios are calculated and stored in the database. These fall into four groups: (1) Ratios describing the operational performance in a specific fiscal year (derived from the gain and loss statement); (2) Ratios describing the financial situation of the company (derived from the balance sheet); (3) Ratios describing the employee's productivity; and (4) Ratios describing other characteristics of the company.

THE HEURISTIC MODEL

Traditional static forms of publications, even when they are posted on the Internet, do not allow the flexibility and interactivity which is necessary to build a system which adapts to individually-varying information needs. One of the major problems encountered in benchmarking studies is the trade-off between the comparability of hotels or restaurants as a result of the classification into various industry sectors/strategic groups and the number of companies that could be used in a given analysis. The more detailed the grouping, the fewer the companies in groups. For instance, requests concerning the database are very specific sometimes, e.g., *"What is the average occupancy rate for an 80 bed hotel-garni in Tyrol?"* Such specific questions cannot usually be processed, since the database does not include a sufficiently large number of such hotels to produce reliable statistics. However, in many cases the user can be provided with data for quite similar hotels that satisfies his needs. In fact, user requests to the AHRP database are frequently very imprecise and sometimes difficult to convert into an exact query.

However, this problem can be solved by a multi-attribute weighting model. This multi-attribute weighting model is an heuristic modelling approach when the weighting factors are derived by expert judgements (Wöber, 1999). The objective of this approach is to introduce a system which could identify similar hotel and restaurant businesses and simultaneously guarantee at least a minimum level of representation decided on by the user.

Recalling the extended transformation model from Figure 1, the main variables identified in this model were the output Y, the discretionary input X^D, and the non-discretionary input X^N. There are several possible ways the relationships between these constructs can be measured and used for the identification of optimal (best practice) comparison partners.

When there seems to be prior knowledge of what is a more favourable environment, caused by X^N combinations, the identification of an optimal comparison partner could be evaluated by finding an optimal $X^{D\rightarrow} Y$ relationship. The investigation of the environmental factors concerns questions such as which factors are decisive and how many industry sectors (markets) must be distinguished. This evaluation is obviously a stratification problem which needs to consider the (discretionary) input/output relationships. Therefore, all methodologies which are capable to handle this clustering problem are relevant for the optimal selection of comparison partners.

The stratification of surveys is in part to form as homogeneous groups as possible that, where numbers allow analysis of a stratum can occur and otherwise, based on estimates of stratum size, the reliability of the information obtained on aggregation is increased. This study proposes six criteria (S) in the weighting approach to establish homogeneity while preserving sample size. The stratification is done on the basis of the type of services offered by the establishments–S_1 (Table 2), the number of days of operation–S_2, the geographical area where the enterprise is located–S_3 (Table 3), the ownership–S_4 (Table 4), the size–S_5 (measured by turnover and number of employees) and the category–S_6 (Table 5).

Selection of the comparability values is a crucial decision because it has a significant influence on the performance of the decision support system. There is no real theory in hospitality research concerning the criteria which determine competitive pressures among hotel and restaurant enterprises. As a result the values had to be assigned by expert judgements in co-operation with the Austrian Professional Hotel and Restaurant Associations and various consultants specialised in hotel and restaurant operations.

TABLE 2. Types of Service Offered by the Establishments

		1	2	3	4	5	6	7
1	Hotel garni	100						
2	Hotel incl. F&B	80	100					
3	Spa hotel	60	80	100				
4	Restaurant	0	50	40	100			
5	Inn, Pub, Tavern	0	40	30	80	100		
6	Cafe house/shop	0	10	0	50	80	100	
7	Espresso/Bar	0	0	0	20	50	80	100

A general comparability equation is suggested in the form of an additive function which also includes an additional weighting procedure to adapt to the situational needs of the user accessing the system. The total weighted comparability value C for each individual enterprise i is:

(1) $$C_i = \sum_{j=1}^{6} S_{ij} w_i$$

The weights for $w_1, \ldots, w_6$ are assigned by the user according to his requirements by a simple scale from 0 to 3 (0 = not important, 1 = less important, 2 = important, 3 = very important).

After rating each establishment represented in the panel database, the enterprises can be easily sorted by their comparability with the user's case. The number of units under evaluation and the homogeneity in the data set are determined by the number of establishments in the sample which will be drawn after this sorting procedure. According to the user's desire in the accuracy of the results, he will specify a high or low number of establishments which will go into the sample file. This trade-off is made explicit by a bi-polar rating scale

TABLE 3. Geographical Area Where the Enterprise Is Located

		1	2	3	4
1	Vienna	100			
2	> 50,000 inhabitants	80	100		
3	15,000-50,000 inhabitants	60	80	100	
4	< 15,000 inhabitants	40	60	80	100

TABLE 4. The Ownership

		1	2
1	Complete ownership	100	
2	Rented or leased	70	100

TABLE 5. The Categorisation Scheme

		1	2	3	4	5
1	*****	100				
2	****	80	100			
3	***	50	80	100		
4	**	30	50	80	100	
5	*	10	30	50	80	100

where the user is able to decide which of the these conflicting objectives has more importance for the decision problem at hand (Figure 3).

In order to keep the programming effort simple, the prototype system uses an integer 9-point-rating (r = 9) to decide on the relation between reliability and similarity. The necessary transformation also considers a minimum sample size (n_{min}) of establishments (e.g., 30) to guarantee a certain level of precision. The actual sample size (n) in accordance to the user's importance of reliability (e) is calculated by

$$n = n_{\min} + \frac{e(N - n_{\min})}{r} \tag{2}$$

where N denotes the total number of establishments in the panel database.

The actual sample size, the user decides by selecting his/her level of reliability, leads to the calculation of mean values of various key ratios. However,

FIGURE 3. The User Decides Whether Comparability or Reliability Is More Important to His Decision Problem

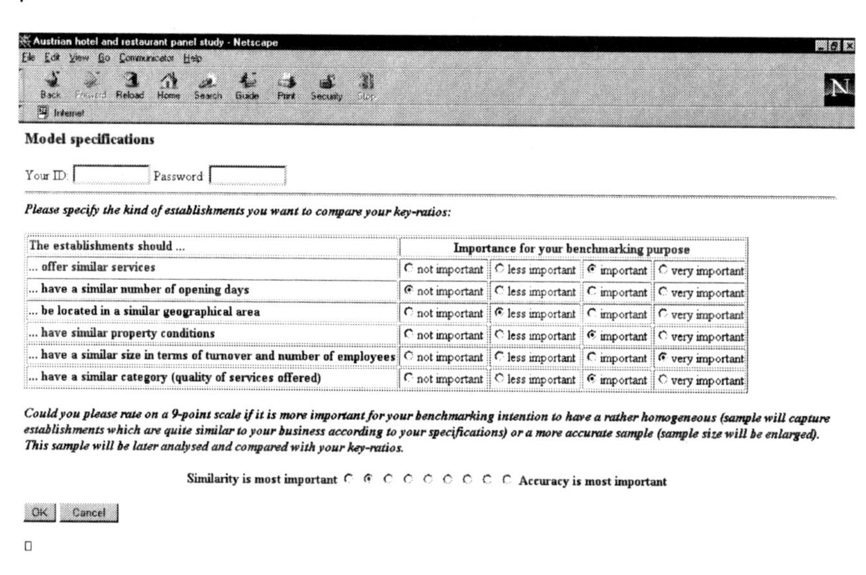

Austrian hotel and restaurant panel study - Netscape

Model specifications

Your ID: Password

Please specify the kind of establishments you want to compare your key-ratios:

The establishments should ...	Importance for your benchmarking purpose			
... offer similar services	not important	less important	(●) important	very important
... have a similar number of opening days	(●) not important	less important	important	very important
... be located in a similar geographical area	not important	(●) less important	important	very important
... have similar property conditions	not important	less important	(●) important	very important
... have a similar size in terms of turnover and number of employees	not important	less important	important	(●) very important
... have a similar category (quality of services offered)	not important	less important	(●) important	very important

Could you please rate on a 9-point scale if it is more important for your benchmarking intention to have a rather homogeneous (sample will capture establishments which are quite similar to your business according to your specifications) or a more accurate sample (sample size will be enlarged). This sample will be later analysed and compared with your key-ratios.

Similarity is most important ○ ● ○ ○ ○ ○ ○ ○ ○ Accuracy is most important

OK Cancel

arithmetic mean or median data are rarely useful without accompanying information. Generally, one would also like to have indication of the variability of the sample or population and the number of observations on which the mean was computed. Such information facilitates the identification of significant differences and, other things being equal, helps define the confidence that one can place in the data.

In principal, the likelihood of variability can easily be calculated when a random sample is taken from a large population. The respondents to the AHRP study, however, form a sample which is not randomly selected but self-selected. There is little that can be done about this except to make every effort to achieve a high response rate. In Austria, some information is available on the structure of the hotel and restaurant industry which is used to weight the sample in order to correct certain sources of bias. For example, in the AHRP study, businesses with more employees tend to participate more frequently in the survey. To correct this misdistribution, information about the real size of hotels and restaurants is used, available through a regular survey of the Austrian Central Statistical Office.

In a random sample generated from a large population, the size of the standard error depends on the size of the sample and is unrelated to the size of the population. For a manager interested in comparing his/her business data with composite figures derived from the database, it is certainly important to have a confidence interval for the estimated industry sector ratio x^* under investigation. For example, when assuming key ratios to be normally distributed, a confidence interval at a 95 percent significance level (a* = .05) can be defined by

$$(3) \quad \bar{x} - 1.96\sqrt{\frac{\sigma^2}{n}} \le x^* \le \bar{x} + 1.96\sqrt{\frac{\sigma^2}{n}} \; \textit{for}\ \alpha = .05,\ \textit{and}\ x \sim N\left[0, \sigma_x^2\right]..$$

The homogeneity of the resulting sample can be expressed by an indicator, derived from equation (1) and expressed in equation (4).

$$(4) \qquad C = \frac{\sum_{i=1}^{n} \sum_{j=1}^{6} S_{ij} w_j}{6n \sum_{j=1}^{6} w_j}$$

The indicator, which is standardised between 0 and 100 (100 = complete similarity with the case example entered by the user; 0 = no comparable establishment found in the total panel data set), is displayed together with the key ratios calculated by the program. This homogeneity indicator helps the manager to understand the composition of the sample and hence supports him/her during the interpretation of the results (Figure 4).

The desired level of precision may be selected by giving the amount of error that someone is willing to tolerate in sample estimates. This amount is determined in light of the uses to which the sample results are to be put. Sometimes it is difficult to decide how much error should be tolerated, particularly when the results have several different uses. In the present application, for instance, an entrepreneur who is interested in opening a new hotel will certainly have completely different information needs in comparison to a manager of an operating establishment. Part of the difficulty is that not enough is known about the consequences of errors of different sample sizes as their effect on the decisions are difficult to observe.

CONCLUSIONS

One of the most challenging tasks in the 21st century is mastering the information explosion, caused in large part by the availability of increasingly so-

FIGURE 4. Sample Output Page of the Hospitality Benchmarking Program

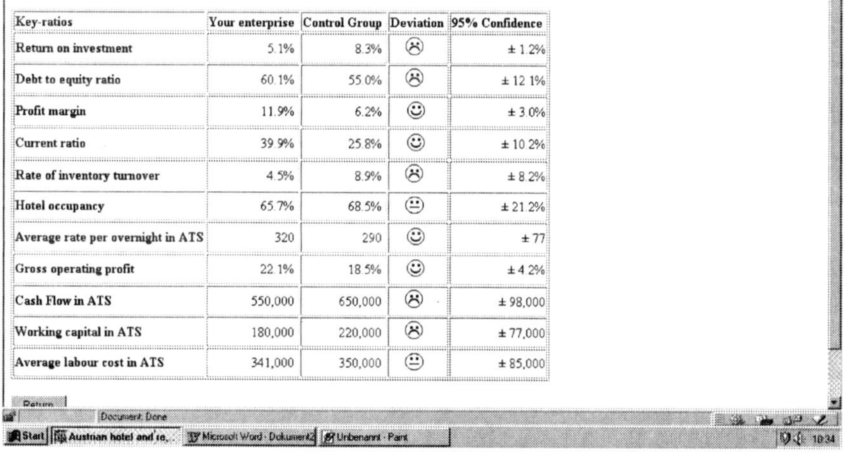

Austrian hotel and restaurant panel study - Netscape

Benchmarking results

Your ID 0346

Homogeneity: 64%
Number of establishments represented in sample file: 125 (10%)

Key-ratios	Your enterprise	Control Group	Deviation	95% Confidence
Return on investment	5.1%	8.3%	☹	± 1.2%
Debt to equity ratio	60.1%	55.0%	☹	± 12.1%
Profit margin	11.9%	6.2%	☺	± 3.0%
Current ratio	39.9%	25.8%	☺	± 10.2%
Rate of inventory turnover	4.5%	8.9%	☹	± 8.2%
Hotel occupancy	65.7%	68.5%	😐	± 21.2%
Average rate per overnight in ATS	320	290	☺	± 77
Gross operating profit	22.1%	18.5%	☺	± 4.2%
Cash Flow in ATS	550,000	650,000	☹	± 98,000
Working capital in ATS	180,000	220,000	☹	± 77,000
Average labour cost in ATS	341,000	350,000	😐	± 85,000

phisticated information processing technology. From the business science perspective, researchers will have to allow themselves to be asked: Are managers getting the information they *need?*

The decision process in the field of financial management involves the analysis of a large volume of data and information (Brignall and Ballantine, 1996:23). Therefore, the need to access large databases and perform computations in real time is vital. This need has led researchers to implement decision support systems in various fields of financial management, such as financial planning, financial analysis and portfolio management. An extensive review of the literature on this subject was recently performed by Zopounidis et al. (1997). However, not a single reference of their 93 entries identifies a publication concerning a financial benchmarking system.

The practice of benchmarking, as detailed by Camp and widely followed by practitioners, is dominated by the search for specific practices that will enhance performance with a controlled allocation of resources. This improved efficiency is achieved by the discovery of specific practices, typically for a single problem area, relying on simple engineering ratios. Typical benchmarking handbooks offer checklists for the conduction of a benchmarking project. These checklists are vaguely defined and sometimes even contradictory in process and content. For example, Camp's original ten-step benchmarking process (Camp, 1989) is described by Watson (1992) in the form of a six-step process.

There is a vast amount of literature on benchmarking in management science, however, most of the studies are pure applications of only limited theoretical value. Very little attention is paid to methodological aspects in conjunction with benchmarking, especially to the right selection of benchmarking partners. Recently, Cross noted that 'one of the major weaknesses of many benchmarking studies is not spending enough time researching which companies might make relevant partners' (Cross, 1998:9). However, the search for leadership companies and functions as introduced by Camp and others appears to be complex and lengthy. Bell and Morey express this well stating: "the identification of leadership companies *[in benchmarking studies]* is as much art as science" (Bell and Morey, 1994:478). Camp recommends the use of consultants, vendors, and functional experts within the organisation seeking help, as well as, industry associations and public databases, as important sources of information for use in the selection of comparative companies. The level of detail provided for the selection of benchmarking partners seems insufficient, especially when compared to the efforts and costs involved in site visits and the implementation of change in the organisation.

The applicability of a heuristic procedure for the identification of benchmarking partners in an interactive database environment was presented by this paper. The advantage of the proposed system is that the user can go back and forth and learn from the output. He/she can change the sample size and therefore the reliability of the results, as well as the criteria which defines on the competitive situation he/she is facing. They are not bound to a strict classification as is usual in ordinary printed publications of panel studies. Hence, the user will realise soon that results may vary significantly, sometimes even through minor changes in his/her preliminary assumptions. Therefore, he/she can gain more insights and a better understanding of how to interpret benchmarking results and how to use them for managerial purposes.

There are several caveats to this heuristic approach in the selection of benchmarking partners by the means of financial key ratios. First, a problem relates to the question whether there is the necessary relation between the homogeneity in the company sample and the number of units derived from the panel database. Decisions on the significance levels of confidence intervals and the necessary preciseness in the benchmarking results have a major impact on this problem. Obviously, the adjustments to get reasonably accurate estimates depend on the underlying application which has to be investigated.

Another problem arises during the weighting process of the various competitive criteria. It is clear that the ideal set of weights depends on the decision problem the user is faced with. However, someone could argue that the user could have difficulty to objectively estimate how relevant this is to their decision problem. In fact, first empirical tests of the prototype program showed that users tend to indicate that all criteria are very important for their benchmarking task. Future improvements of the system could incorporate an evaluation of the various decision problems and perform a self-determination of the weighting values. Therefore, poor or irrelevant weights by users could be replaced by system values fed back to users.

REFERENCES

Anderson, R.I., Fish, M., Xia, Y. and Michello, F. (1999) Measuring Efficiency in the Hotel Industry: A Stochastic Frontier Approach. *Hospitality Management*, 18(1), 45-57.

Anderson, R.I., Fok, R. and Scott J. (2000) Hotel Industry Efficiency: An Advanced Linear Programming Examination. *American Business Review* (January), 40-48.

Athanassopoulos, A.D. and Curram, S.P. (1996) A Comparison of Data Envelopment Analysis and Artificial Neural Networks as Tools for Assessing the Efficiency of Decision Making Units. *Journal of the Operational Research Society*, 47(August), 1000-1016.

Bell, R.A. and Morey, R.C. (1994) The Search for Appropriate Benchmarking Partners: A Macro Approach and Application to Corporate Travel Management. *Omega, International Journal of Management Science*, 22(5), 477-490.

Boger, C.A., Cai, L.A. and Lin, Li-C. (1999) Benchmarking: Comparing Discounted Business Rates Among Lodging Companies. *Journal of Hospitality and Tourism Research*, 23(3), 256-267.

Bottomley, V. (1995) *Tourism: Competing With the Best. Benchmarking for Smaller Hotels*. KPMG study, Department of National Heritage, London.

Breiter, D. and Kline, S.F. (1995) Benchmarking Quality Management in Hotels. *FIU Hospitality Review*, 13(2), 45-60.

Brignall, S. and Ballantine, J. (1996) Performance Measurement in Service Businesses Revisited. *International Journal of Service Industry Management*, 7(1), 6-31.

Camp, R.C. (1989) *Benchmarking: The Search For Industry Best Practices That Lead To Superior Performance*. Milwaukee, WI: American Society for Quality Control Quality Press.

Cross, M. (1998) *The Benchmarking Sourcebook*. London: Batsford Ltd.

Cubbin, J. and Tzanidakis, G. (1998) Techniques for Analysing Company Performance. *Business Strategy Review*, 9(4), 37-46.

Dubé, L., Enz, C.A., Renaghan, L.M. and Siguaw, J.A. (1999) *American Lodging Excellence: The Key to Best Practices in the U.S. Lodging Industry*. American Express and the American Hotel Foundation, Washington, DC.

Durocher, J.F. and Niman, N.B. (1993) Information Technology: Management Effectiveness and Guest Services. *Hospitality Research Journal*, 17(1), 121-131.

Geller, A.N. (1985) The Current State of Hotel Information Systems. *Cornell Hotel & Restaurant Administration Quarterly*, 25(2), 14-17.

Go, F.M. and Pine, R. (1995) *Globalisation Strategy in the Hotel Industry*. Routledge, London.

Halachmi, A. (2000) Information Technology and Performance Measurement: Promise or Peril? *National Productivity Review*, 19(3), 87-93.

Harris, P.J. and Brown, J.B. (1998) Research and Development in Hospitality Accounting and Financial Management. *International Journal of Hospitality Management*, 17(2), 161-181.

Horwath International (1998) *World-Wide Hotel Industry Study*. Horwath International, Coral Gables, FL.

Kirk, D. and Pine, R. (1998) Research in Hospitality Systems and Technology. *International Journal of Hospitality Management*, 17(2), 203-217.

Kluge, E.A. (1996) A Literature Review of Information Technology in the Hospitality Curriculum. *Hospitality Research Journal*, 19(4), 45-64.

Kozak, M. and Rimmington, M. (1998) Benchmarking: Destination Attractiveness and Small Hospitality Business Performance. *International Journal of Contemporary Hospitality Management*, 10(5), 184-188.

Min, H. and Min, H. (1997) Benchmarking the Quality of Hotel Services: Managerial Perspectives. *International Journal of Quality & Reliability Management*, 14(6), 582-597.

Monkhouse, E. (1995) The Role of Competitive Benchmarking in Small-to Medium-Sized Enterprises. *Benchmarking for Quality Management & Technology*, 2(4), 41-50.

Morey, R.C. and Dittman, D.A. (1995) Evaluating a Hotel GM's Performance. A Case Study in Benchmarking. *Cornell Hotel and Restaurant Administration Quarterly*, 36(5), 30-35.

Motwani, J., Kumar, A. and Youssef, M.A. (1996) Implementing Quality Management in the Hospitality Industry: Current Efforts and Future Research Directions. *Benchmarking for Quality Management & Technology*, 3(4), 4-17.

Pannell Kerr Forster (1998) *A Review of the Hotel Sector in Copenhagen Compared to Selected European Competitor Cities*. Danish Tourist Board, Copenhagen.

Phillips, P.A. (1996a) Strategic Planning and Business Performance in the Quoted UK Hotel Sector: Results of an Exploratory Study. *International Journal of Hospitality Management*, 15(4), 347-362.

Phillips, P.A. (1996b) *Organisational Strategy, Strategic Planning Systems Characteristics, and Business Performance in the UK Hotel Sector*. PhD thesis, Cardiff Business School, Cardiff University, Wales.

Phillips, P.A. and Appiah-Adu, K. (1998) Benchmarking to Improve the Strategic Planning Process in the Hotel Sector. *The Service Industries Journal*, 18(1), 1-18.

Phillips, P.A. and Moutinho, L. (1998a) The marketing planning index: A Tool for Measuring Strategic Marketing Effectiveness. *Journal of Travel and Tourism Marketing*, 7(3), 41-60.

Phillips, P.A. and Moutinho, L. (1998b) *Strategic Planning Systems in Hospitality and Tourism*. CABI Publishing, Wallingford.

Phillips, P.A. and Moutinho, L. (1999) Measuring Strategic Planning Effectiveness in Hotels. *International Journal of Contemporary Hospitality Management*, 11(7), 349-358.

Siguaw, J.A. and Enz, C.A. (1999a) Best Practices in Marketing. *Cornell Hotel and Restaurant Administration Quarterly*, 40(5), 31-43.

Siguaw, J.A. and Enz, C.A. (1999b) Best Practices in Food and Beverage Management. *Cornell Hotel and Restaurant Administration Quarterly*, 40(5), 50-57.

Siguaw, J.A. and Enz, C.A. (1999c) Best Practices in Hotel Operations. *Cornell Hotel and Restaurant Administration Quarterly*, 40(6), 42-53.

Spendolini, M.J. (1992) *The Benchmarking Book*. New York, NY: Amacom.

Sundgaard, E., Rosenberg, L. and Johns, N. (1998) A Typology of Hotels as Individual Players: The Case of Bornholm, Nexoe, Denmark. *International Journal of Contemporary Hospitality Management*, 10(5), 180-183.

Thanassoulis, E., Boussofiane, A. and Dyson, R.G. (1996) A Comparison of Data Envelopment Analysis and Ratio Analysis as Tools for Performance Assessment. *Omega, International Journal of Management Science*, 24(3), 229-244.

Umbreit, W.T. and Eder, R.W. (1987) Linking Hotel Manager Behaviour with Outcome Measures of Effectiveness. *International Journal of Hospitality Management* 6(3), 139-147.

Watson, G.H. (1992) *The Benchmarking Workbook: Adapting Best Practices for Performance Improvement*. Portland, OR: Productivity Press.

Wöber, K. (1999) Comparing Operating Ratios for Small and Medium Hotel and Restaurant Businesses: A decision support system using Internet technology. In Buhalis, D. and Schertler, W. (eds.) *Information and Communication Technologies in Tourism*. Springer, Wien, pp. 238-246.

Wöber, K. (2000a) *Betriebskennzahlen des Österreichischen Gastgewerbes. Bilanzjahr 1992(-1998)*. Österreichischer Wirtschaftsverlag, Wien. (Note: regularly published since 1994.)

Wöber, K.W. (2000b) Benchmarking Hotel Operations on the Internet: A Data Envelopment Analysis Approach. *Information Technology and Tourism*, 3(3/4), 195-212.

Zairi, M. (1996) *Benchmarking for Best Practice: Continuous Learning Through Sustainable Innovation*. Oxford: Butterworth-Heinemann.

Zopounidis, C., Doumpos, M. and Matsatsinis, N.F. (1997) On the Use of Knowledge-Based Decision Support Systems in Financial Management: A Survey. *Decision Support Systems*, 20(3), 259-277.

Development Opportunities for a Tourism Benchmarking Tool–The Case of Tyrol

Matthias Fuchs
Klaus Weiermair

SUMMARY. The aim of this study is to improve an already existing Tourism benchmarking tool designed and implemented by the Austrian Provincial Government of Tyrol in 1987 (Haemmerle and Lehar 1987, Berktold 1992). After a brief introduction which overviews latest benchmarking approaches within tourism (Morey and Dittman 1995, Kozak and Rimmington 1998, Siguaw and Enz 1999, Dubé et al. 1999, Ritchie and Crouch 2000) and emphasizing its strategic significance of continually monitoring and emulating standards of performance, the principal purpose of an already existing benchmarking tool, the Tyrolean Tourism Barometer, is described in form of a case study. Both, the data gathering process as well as the operational sequences leading to a variety of indicators are thoroughly discussed. The paper concludes by analyzing the strengths and weaknesses of this secondary data based benchmarking tool. The final section of the paper critically assesses the neglect of relevant elements within the production process of tourism

Matthias Fuchs is Assistant Professor, Center for Tourism and Service Economics, University of Innsbruck, Universitätsstraße 15, A-6020 Innsbruck (E-mail: matthias.fuchs@uibk.ac.at).

Klaus Weiermair is Professor and Head of the Center of Tourism and Service Economics, University of Innsbruck, Universitätsstraße 15, A-6020 Innsbruck (E-mail: klaus.weiermair@uibk.ac.at).

[Haworth co-indexing entry note]: "Development Opportunities for a Tourism Benchmarking Tool–The Case of Tyrol." Fuchs, Matthias, and Klaus Weiermair. Co-published simultaneously in *Journal of Quality Assurance in Hospitality & Tourism* (The Haworth Hospitality Press, an imprint of The Haworth Press, Inc.) Vol. 2, No. 3/4, 2001, pp. 71-91; and: *Benchmarks in Hospitality and Tourism* (ed: Sungsoo Pyo) The Haworth Hospitality Press, an imprint of The Haworth Press, Inc., 2001, pp. 71-91. Single or multiple copies of this article are available for a fee from The Haworth Document Delivery Service [1-800-HAWORTH, 9:00 a.m. - 5:00 p.m. (EST). E-mail address: getinfo@haworthpressinc.com].

services. Here, the point will be made that it will not suffice to only describe structural shifts in tourism supply and demand in order to establish a reliable instrument for retrospectively evaluating tourism policy and strategically optimize future destination policies. Thus, the existing approach, initially based on price and capacity data only, is extended by linking it to both quality measures of customer satisfaction as well as resource allocation conditions (Weiermair and Fuchs 1999, Wöber 2000).

KEYWORDS. Destination benchmarking, tool development, destination management, alpine tourism

INTRODUCTION

Benchmarking is often defined as the search for best industry practices which lead to top performance (Camp 1995, p 3); consequently, some authors identified its benefits for an organization fourfold as showing organizations how to better meet customer needs, identifying their strengths and weaknesses, stimulating the continuous operational improvement and finally creating innovative ideas in a cost-effective way (Smith et al. 1993, Karlof and Ostblom 1994). Indeed, in management science today benchmarking is positioned as representing an extension of an existing total quality program or as being a procedure to establish new, more relevant and efficient standards of performance (Leibried and McNair 1992, Wöber 2000b). So far, benchmarking studies have been applied most notably to the manufacturing industry by stressing the link to total quality management (Spendolini 1992, Cook 1995). Moreover, while benchmarking applications are growing substantially in large organizations, they have had as yet limited application among small hospitality businesses in recent years (Kozac and Rimmington 1998, p. 184).

The few existing examples of benchmarking within the tourism industry are mainly those involving hotel operations (Morey and Dittman 1995, Bottomley 1995, Boger et al. 1999) and/or applications in food and beverage management (Siguaw and Enz 1999a). A number of best practices could also be found in the field of tourism marketing (Breiter and Kline 1995). For instance, within its benchmark group consisting of 18 hotels, *ACCOR* developed three strategic categories which are thought to account for the development of total performance (Siguaw 1999b, p. 37). Tourist expectations and quality perceptions have also been analyzed within a benchmarking framework, with some authors investigating the functional areas affecting the creation of a positive customer value (Johns et al. 1996, Dubé et al 1999). For instance, Dubé et al. (1999) identified three most significant fields for a worry-free hotel overnight stay, such as personnel, check-in/check-out standards and brand/reputation correspondence (Dubé et al. 1999). Furthermore, Weiermair and Fuchs (1998/99) deciphered highly influential tourist activities and quality dimensions affecting quality assessments on destinations by verifying the existence of a linear relationship between an overall quality measure and partial quality assessments related to different quality dimensions and tourism activities, respectively. In their benchmark case study of 11 wintersport resorts they found that shopping and sport activities others than skiing and the quality dimensions of variety/fun and freedom of choice contributed most to the formation of an overall quality judgment with respect to destinations (Fuchs and Weiermair 1998, Weiermair and Fuchs, 1999). Recently, highly valuable benchmarking studies were performed within the context of destinations (Ritchie and Crouch 2000, Go and Govers 2000, Murphy et al. 2000). For instance, Go and Govers (2000) present results of eight best practice case studies of different destinations in four European countries in order to demonstrate that integrated quality management in tourist destinations was rather underdeveloped with the only exception of destination policy and/or strategy management elements (Go and Govers 2000, p. 79). Furthermore, Kozak and Rimmington (1998) have argued that there is considerable potential for improving service quality by means of benchmarking not only within the small tourism business sector, but also within tourist destinations as consumers can benefit from clearer indications of the services likely to be offered, so that their service expectations are likely to correspond more closely with performance and which in turn will increase their satisfaction with the destination (Kozak and Rimmington 1998, p. 184).

An often quoted source of misconception in the research field of benchmarking is the difference between benchmarking techniques and competitive analyses. As the idea of benchmarking basically comes from examining the gap between own and others' performance levels it must be clearly distinguished from the traditional form of competitive analysis which mainly focuses on the competitor's strategic market activity and does not have the purpose to study why and how competitors (i.e., best-of-class organizations) act. Nevertheless, mainly for the optimal selection of comparison partners for benchmark studies, some authors note the high importance to conduct preliminary competitive analyses (Zairi 1996, Wöber 2000b). For this special purpose a number of more or less sophisticated empirical tools have been developed in the economic literature. A relatively simple but highly valuable example presents the *shift-share analysis*. This method, in the meantime also used in the tourism literature, works with easily-accessible quantitative data (e.g., tourist arrivals, tourism spendings) and may be considered as a very helpful tool in the first phases of a market opportunity analysis, as its results inform decision makers about the relative competitive advantage of their destination (Sirakaya et al. 1995, Fuchs et al. 2000).

The aim of this paper is to present an already existing benchmarking tool which had originally been designed and implemented by the Austrian Provincial Government of Tyrol in 1987 in order to extend the National Statistics beyond time series for deciphering quantitative dimensions of tourism development over time (i.e., overnight stays, price levels and/or tourism occupancy rates). As the tool is theoretically derived within the benchmarking framework, the *"Tyrolean Tourism Barometer"* shows both elements of a benchmarking tool as well as features of competitive analysis techniques allowing also to monitor qualitative aspects of tourism development within a prespecified benchmark area. After a thoroughly detailed tool-discussion the final part of the paper attempts to provide new insights into development opportunities/directions for more specific tourist destination benchmarking applications.

OBJECTIVES OF THE TYROLEAN TOURISM BAROMETER

Tourism plays a highly important role for the Tyrolean industry. Actually, the GDP's tourism portion stands at 10.8 per cent, whereas the same figure is about 3.5 per cent for Austria as a whole (Mayerhuber et al. 1998). In order to get a broader and more detailed information base to strategically assist this leading branch of economic activity through appropriate tourism policies, the *Tyrolean Tourism Barometer* was introduced in 1987 by the Tyrolean Tourist Board and the Provincial Government of Tyrol (Amt der Tiroler Landesregierung 1987).

Yet, Tyrol has not been the only tourism region in Austria to do so. The Tourism Board of Vorarlberg (Austria) also introduced another Tourism Barometer in 1981 with the aim to obtain meaningful information on the qualitative development of its destinations, being the first European tourism region to have introduced a comprehensive monitoring tool for the importance and role of quality factors in determining general tourism development. The calculated indicators take mainly into consideration *added value, job generation, tax revenues* and *income distribution effects* (Vorarlberg Tourismus 1999). This barometer concept, however, not only requires very detailed information about sales and prices for tourist accommodations but has to also process money exchange data on transactions of tourists in local banks of the tourist region (Haemmerle and Lehar 1987, p. 2). The latter data source will be lost with the introduction of the *EURO* in 2002. Thereafter, besides credit card payments and Non-European currencies, further data of international remittances regarding tourist traffic must be registered. Thus, one of the main reasons why the Tyrolean Tourist Board decided *not* to follow this approach was the fact that Tyrol has three times as many tourism resorts and tourism accommodation facilities, respectively, and four times greater bed capacities than its neighbouring province of Vorarlberg. In other words, it was simply not feasible to copy this benchmarking approach for Tyrol due to the larger amount of necessary data.

The core objective of the Tyrolean Tourism Barometer was and still is the quality improvement of Tyrol's tourism development. One wanted to introduce methods to analyse quality properties within and between tourism destinations. The steady decline and/or the stagnation in *overnight stays* in Tyrol since 1981 added another important dimension to this decision (Tschurtschenthaler 1998, p. 16). As tourism *receipts* (i.e., turnovers) did not decline at the same rate, the observation was made, that, at least tendentially, shifts of tourism demand towards higher priced tourism services must have occured, a trend for quality which couldn't have been quantified as yet. Thus, the target of the Tyrolean Tourism Barometer may be best described as the *monetary evaluation of structural shifts in tourism supply and demand with regard to different regional areas (i.e., destinations).* Consequently, derived indicators such as the turnover index and bed utilization rates are still being used, but figures on structural shifts in tourism demand towards higher-qualitity tourism services (showing the most significant discrepancies for different destinations and/or tourism products) now become more and more important. Moreover, a system of indicators which permits the consecutive evaluation of this development process should ideally meet the following basic requirements (Haemmerle and Lehar 1987):

- Representativity for the Tyrolean tourism industry to reach a maximum of validity and reliability with respect to the chosen indicators
- Quick availability of the benchmark results within a relatively short period of time
- Consideration of spatial variance due to locational dis-/advantages of Tyrolean destinations

Methodological Issues

To meet the above mentioned requirements, the *Tyrolean Tourism Barometer* only uses two data intputs. One variable quantifies tourism demand, namely overnight stays and another variable measures corresponding price developments. Thus, the measurement procedure may be seen as a relatively simple one and may also be considered as strongly tied to the official *overnight statistics,* thereby excluding one-day excursions and other types of transit tourism activities. This approach can be justified on account of the fact that the total turnover volume of the Tyrolean accommodation sector is central to the tourism industry in that it includes more than a half of all regional tourism spendings. Moreover, such an analytical approach is valuable because tourism receipts for sales in tourism-related activities (e.g., for sport activities, transportation, food etc.) are closely tied to the spending for accommodation services, which therefore can be defined as the "tourism core services" (Haemmerle and Lehar 1987, p. 5). In order to obtain necessary *price data* and in contrast to the *Vorarlberger Tourism Barometer,* secondary data sources are employed. Room price lists for each accommodation category and so-called price catalogues published by the regional Tourist Board serve as principal and relatively precise instruments to provide relevant data referring to the prices for overnight stays and breakfast and/or half-board, respectively (i.e., "tourism core services").

Preparation of the Analysis

Data gathering for all of the existing 278 Tyrolean tourism communities with the help of an universal census approach was considered as fairly impossible due to a large volume of data. Therefore, a representative sampling technique based on a-priori elaborated groups of tourism communities was chosen as the most adequate data gathering approach (Everitt 1980, Krug et al. 1994). In order to define structurally similar destination units, the Tyrolean Tourist Board decided to use cluster analysis as a statistical tool which can systematically combine statistical units on account of their similarity based on multivariate profiles. Thus, the study is built upon a matrix investigating 278 different Tyrolean tourism communities and 19 cluster-variables to best characterize and distinguish tourism destinations (Amt der Tiroler Landesregierung 1987, p. 3). It is essential to theoretically operationalize those variables as exactly as possible which permit a reasonable and meaningful cluster building process (Kaufmann and Pape 1984, p. 391). Put differently, the main objective of this preparatory task is to cover all of the relevant structural conditions of tourism development in Tyrol in order to reveal the underlying dynamics of tourism demand. The time series data for the 19 selected cluster-variables were provided by the Austrian National Statistical Office and are summarized in Table 1.

The *Mahalanobis* approach (Punj and Stewart 1983) was used to eliminate possible biases associated with differences in the scales of the selected 19 variables which were employed in the multivariate analysis. Thus, both, standard-

TABLE 1. Cluster-Variables to Classify 278 Tyrolean Tourism Communities

1.	Overnight stays per community
2.	Overnight stays per inhabitant
3.	Overnight stays development (time series from 1976/77 to 1984/85)
4.	Overnight stays development / winter half-year (time series from 1976/77 to 1984/85)
5.	Share of overnight stays / winter half-year
6.	Share of overnight stays in commercial accommodation
7.	Share of overnight stays in A1/A hotel facilities
8.	Bed occupancy rate/ summer half-year
9.	Bed occupancy rate/ winter half-year
10.	Tourists´ length of stay / summer half-year
11.	Tourists´ length of stay / winter half-year
12.	Share of overnight stays of the three most important nations (i.e. Germany, the Netherlands and United Kingdom)
13.	Share of overnight stays of guests from Germany
14.	Share of overnight stays in the peak season during summer
15.	Share of overnight stays in the low season during winter
16.	Number of cable cars, ski-lifts, chair-lifts, mountain railways etc.
17.	Capacity of cable cars, ski-lifts, chair-lifts, mountain railways etc. per community
18.	Share of skiing area per community
19.	Beverage tax per inhabitant

ization as well as adjustments for intercorrelations among the variables is provided by this measure of similarity (Hair et al. 1995, p. 434). The objective of the first step within this clustering process was a definition of the optimal number of clusters followed by the assignment of the statistical units (i.e., the 278 tourism commounities) according to a prespecified measure of similarity. A hierarchical clustering procedure, e.g., the *Centroid method,* the results of which typically are less affected by outliers than are other hierarchical methods, was employed, displaying *eight* differing clusters as optimal (McIntyre and Blashfield 1980). Subsequently, this eight-cluster solution served as the base for a refined version by applying the non-hierarchical *k-means*-clustering algorithm (Hair et al. 1995, p. 440). The final stage of the analysis involved "interpretation" by describing and profiling the main characteristics of each destination-cluster so as to comprehensively explain how they significantly differ on relevant dimensions. Since inception of the Tyrolean Tourism Barometer in 1987, the distribution of the cluster profile among the eight categorized destination types, shown in Table 2, has remained very stable over time (Berktold 1992).

TABLE 2. Cluster Profile of the Eight Destination Types

No.	Destination Type	Number of communities	%	Total overnight stays %	Overnight stays winter half-year %
1	Capital City of Tyrol (e.g. Innsbruck)	1	0.4	3.7	5.5
2	Tourism centres	9	3.2	21.2	25.0
3	Destinations with intensive tourism	20	7.2	19.5	20.9
4	Destinations with intensive winter tourism	34	12.2	15.7	17.7
5	Destinations with intensive summer tourism	76	27.3	23.0	20.6
6	Destinations with city and transit tourism	20	7.2	6.9	4.8
7	Destinations with extensive summer/transit tourism	48	17.3	4.4	2.7
8	Destinations with extensive summer tourism	70	25.2	5.6	2.8
	Total	**278**	**100.0**	**100.0**	**100.0**

Source: adapted from Amt der Tiroler Landeregierung 1987, p. 12

The Survey Approach

The previous chapter illustrated the many steps which are necessary to structure the statistical data base before starting the analysis. When the survey was realised for the first time in 1987, a *multi-stratified* random-sample was drawn. As a result, 55 destinations, or 20 per cent of the total Tyrolean tourism communities, emerged as an optimal sample size (Haemmerle and Lehar 1987, p. 6). Five years later, in 1992, the sample size was slightly increased to 86 communities (i.e., 31 per cent) reaching about 8,000 accommodation units covering 70 percent of the total bed capacity and almost 75 per cent of the Tyrolean overnight stays (Berktold 1992, p. 76). Thus, the used sample should present a broad statistical base and compared to the total Tyrolean population implies a well proportioned sample-distribution. Furthermore, the significance of communities regarding different locational aspects can be taken into account. For example, *4-stars*-hotels (i.e., *A*-category type accommodations) offer varying prices which may be functionally related to the images and prestige-levels of destinations in which they are situated (Sinclair and Stabler 1997, p. 72).

Analysis

Following the results of this preparatory work, both, the matrices for overnight stays as well as price matrices used in the analysis are further subdivided into six accommodation categories and eight destination types (i.e., clustered communities). Initially, *average* prices for "tourism core services" (i.e., overnight stays, breakfasts and/or half-board) were calculated by weighting them with the sales volume of the accommodation units in the sample. Subsequently, a Lespeyres type price index, average price levels per accommodation category and average price levels per destination type were obtained by weighting actual prices with sales figures from previous seasons. The index-calculation procedures are displayed in Figure 1 and 2.

The calculation of benchmark indicators on the basis of previously established index measures may be considered as the final methodological step,

FIGURE 1. Derivation of the price matrix.

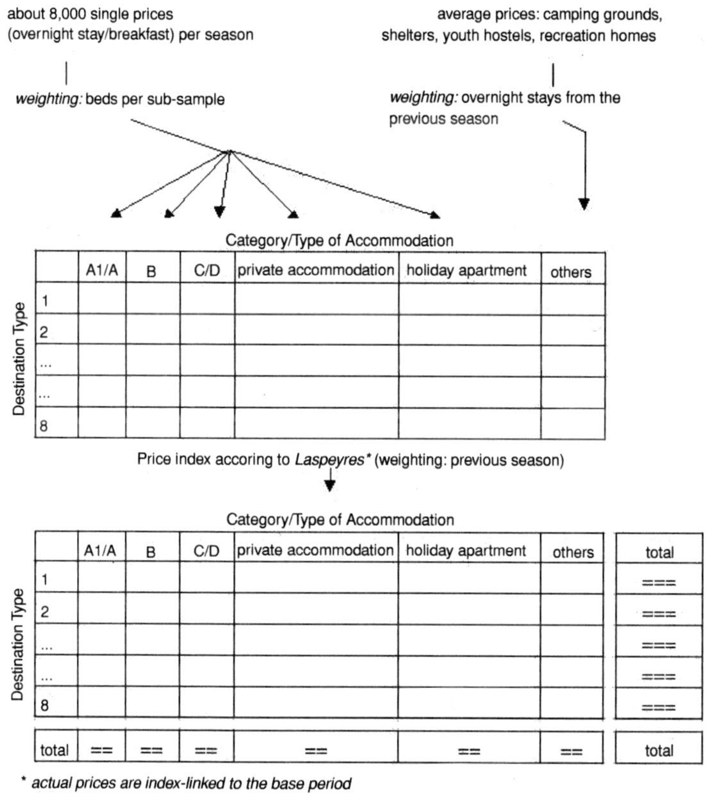

about 8,000 single prices (overnight stay/breakfast) per season

weighting: beds per sub-sample

average prices: camping grounds, shelters, youth hostels, recreation homes

weighting: overnight stays from the previous season

Category/Type of Accommodation

Destination Type	A1/A	B	C/D	private accommodation	holiday apartment	others
1						
2						
...						
...						
8						

Price index accoring to *Laspeyres** (weighting: previous season)

Category/Type of Accommodation

Destination Type	A1/A	B	C/D	private accommodation	holiday apartment	others	total
1							===
2							===
...							===
...							===
8							===
total	==	==	==	==	==	==	total

* *actual prices are index-linked to the base period*

Source: adapted from Berktold 1992, p. 79

FIGURE 2. Derivation of indices.

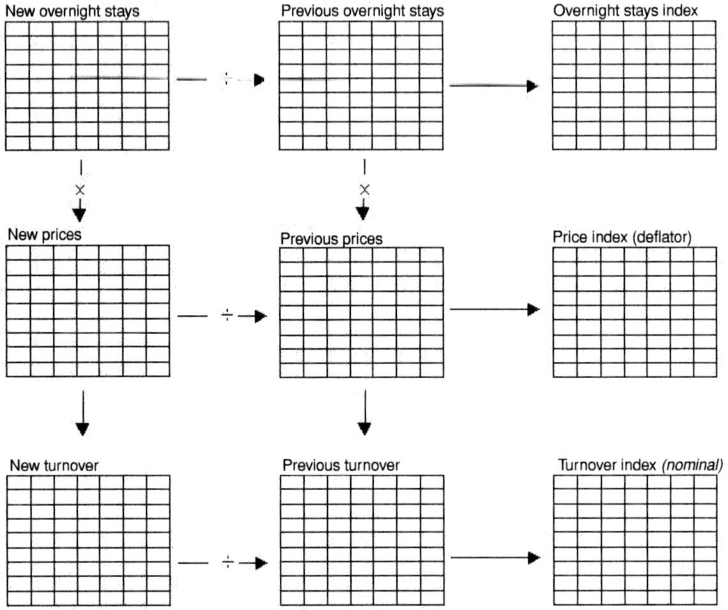

New overnight stays — ÷ → Previous overnight stays → Overnight stays index

New prices — ÷ → Previous prices → Price index (deflator)

New turnover — ÷ → Previous turnover → Turnover index *(nominal)*

Source: adapted from Berktold 1992, p. 80

whereas the underlying general estimation model has been formulated by the following equation (Bertktold 1992, p. 77):

$$\textbf{Turnover Index}_{(real)} = \textbf{Overnight Stays Index} \times \textbf{Price Index} \times \textbf{Quality Index}$$

In practice, simply dividing the turnover index $_{(real)}$ by the overnight stays index leads to residuals which can only be used for obtaining cumulative column and row values of the price matrices (Berktold 1992). It can be shown that the quality index remains a purely theoretical construct and serves as a residual-term to solve the displayed equation above. Put differently, the constructed quality index shows how much turnover would have changed since the previous season, if no structural shifts had emerged, indicating qualitative shifts, both, between accommodation categories within a particular destination (i.e., *category/accommodation type effect*) as well as between destinations with regard to the according accommodation type (i.e., *destination type effect*). Finally, calculations can be prepared also for the entire total Tyrolean benchmark area. The formalized computation of this quality index is summarized in Figure 3.

Empirical Results

As already discussed, the general model structure of the Tyrolean Tourism Barometer allows the calculation of different indicators. First of all, the development of the aggregate benchmark may be decomposed by its structural shifts. For instance, the data for the winter half-year 1989/90 display a decline of 2.9 per cent in overnight stays, while the accommodation sector of Tyrol still manages a minimal increase in turnover of 1.8 per cent (see Figure 4). Due to a relatively faster price increase in 1989/90, the real turnover index is negative, standing at –2.6 per cent. Thus, the positive difference between the latter index and the change in overnight stays (i.e., 0.3) may be interpreted as a small shift towards higher quality in tourism services. In other words, about 10 per cent of the losses on account of the drop in overnight stays was "picked up" by a qualitative shift in demand (see Figure 4).

FIGURE 3. Derivation of the quality index.

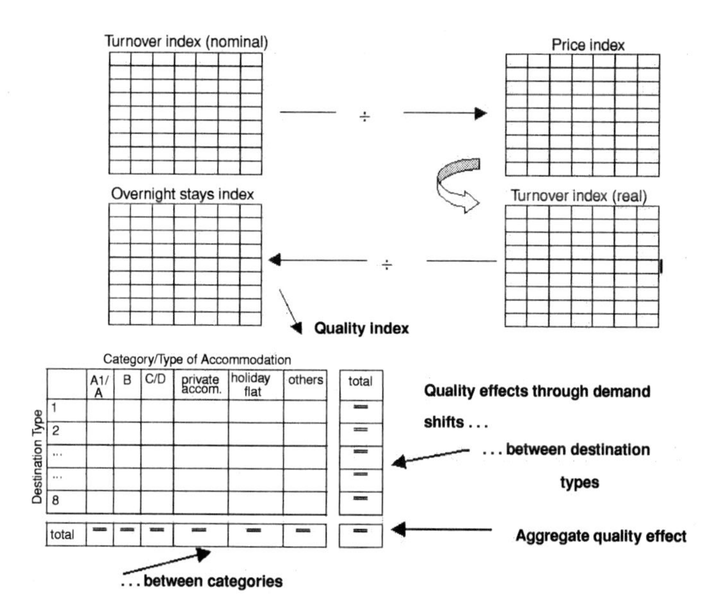

Source: adapted from Berktold 1992, p. 81

The most recent patterns of shifts may be interpreted in a similar way. For the winter half-year 1999/2000 the traditional demand indicator of overnight stays, stood at 3.3 per cent, with a real turnover index amounting to 5.1 per cent. Thus, for the last winters' total tourism performance, the benchmark area of Tyrol was showing both quantitative as well as qualitative improvements (see Figure 4).

More detailed and also more valuable information for both, destination managers as well as tourism policy makers can further be obtained by analyzing shift patterns of tourism demand with special regard to different destination types and/or accommodation categories. First of all, a highly concentrated and also mostly time invariant "market structure" of the benchmark area becomes evident. For instance, for the winter half-year 1999/2000 it can be shown that 33.4 per cent of all overnight stays (corresponding to a share of almost 44 per cent of the total turnover) were realized in tourism centres (i.e., destination type 2), whereas its share of all Tyrolean communities is falling at only 3.2 per cent. Table 3 depicts the *Tyrolean Tourism Barometer's* output screen for that year summarizing the most important shift indicators of tourism demand for eight destination types and six different accommodation categories, respectively.

By quantifying the so-called *destination type effect* demand shifts between different destination types can be analyzed. First of all, widely varying price

FIGURE 4. Aggregate benchmark data over time.

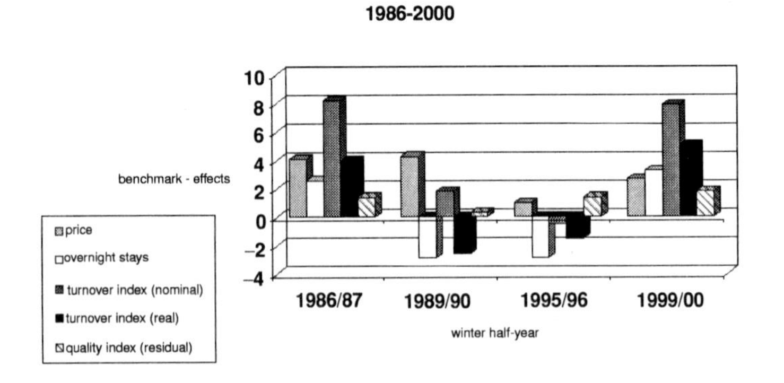

Source: kindly provided by Amt der Tiroler Landeregierung, Department of Statistics, 2001

TABLE 3. The Tyrolean Tourism Barometer 1999/2000

	changes in per cent (%) winter half-year 1999/00 versus 1999/98					share in per cent (%)		turnovers in
	prices	overnight stays	turnover (nom.)	turnover (real)	quality index	overnight stays	turnovers	mill. EURO
destination type/accommodation category								
capital (i.e. Innsbruck)	4,4	0,3	8,4	3,8	3,5	2	2,9	25,530
tourism centre	3,3	5,6	10,5	7	1,4	33,4	43,9	382,877
dest. with intensive tourism	0,8	2,5	5	4,2	1,6	20,1	20,3	177,409
dest. with intensive winter tourism	4,3	3,8	8,2	3,7	–0,1	16,1	12,8	111,691
dest. with intensive summer tourism	2,7	1,7	6,7	3,8	2,1	21,2	15,5	135,055
dest. with city and transit tourism	2,5	–3,2	1,7	–0,8	2,4	1,7	1,3	11,388
dest. with extensive summer/transit tourism	0,7	–0,4	–0,7	–1,4	–1	2,5	1,8	15,349
dest. with extensive summer tourism	1,5	1,5	2,4	0,9	–0,6	3	1,6	13,597
category A/A1	3,2	7,1	11,1	7,3	0,2	24,3	48,5	423,152
category B	3,6	5,2	8,2	5,4	0,2	21,3	22,2	193,382
category C/D	2,7	–4,6	–1,6	–4,5	0,1	18,2	11,9	104,147
holiday apartment	2,2	35,9	37,4	34,5	–1,1	6,8	4,1	35,813
private accommodation	0,3	–1,4	–0,8	–1	0,4	25,8	12,2	107,105
others	0,3	–2,1	–1,8	–2,1	0	3,6	1,1	9,353
TYROL (i.e. benchmark area)	**2,7**	**3,3**	**7,9**	**5,1**	**1,7**	**100**	**100**	**872,953**

Source: kindly provided by Amt der Tiroler Landeregierung, Department of Statisitics, 2001

levels among destinations are pointed out. While for those tourism communities which are characterized by rather extensive tourism revenues (i.e., destination types 7 and 8) prices only rose by approximately 1.5 per cent, in destinations with *intensive* winter tourism (i.e., type 4) prices rose by 4.3 per cent (see table 3). For the latter destination type this was also the main reason why they show a slightly falling quality effect. Moreover, prices don't only correlate with the destination type but there is enough evidence to suggest that price levels are significantely higher in the winter season. To be more precise, on average tourism price levels are about 26 per cent higher in the winter half-years than during the summer season. Thus, it may be argued that price differences between winter and summer are not only derived from higher fixed-costs (e.g., heating, warm water) but that they are also "market driven" due to higher profit margins during the winter half-year. Viewed differently, higher price levels also reflect the greater attractiveness of winter holidays in the alpine regions of Austria. If we assume that communities with city and/or transit tourism (i.e., destination type 6) can in the winter season only charge a markup for the heating costs, the difference to all of the others destinations' price levels could therefore be regarded as a rough estimate for average locational rents. These figures, ranging from 28 per cent for tourism centres (destination type 2) to a mere 4 per cent for communities with extensive summer-and transit tourism (destination type 7) are important data for tourism policy decisions. They may also enhance the willingness of weaker destinations to cooperate with other stronger and more competitive destinations. In an analogous fashion, the *accommodation type effect* (i.e., *category effect*) can quantify shifts in demand between different accommodation catagories by making empirically evident the ongoing trend towards high-standard overnight stays (i.e., category *A1/A* or *B*) compared to the low-standard type (i.e., category *C/D*) and/or compared to the private accommodation sector (see Table 3).

Finally, two further types of indicators can be provided by the Tyrolean benchmarking tool and are worthy to further discussion. The basic idea of the Tyrolean Tourism Barometer, namely the weighting of demand units (i.e., overnight stays) through its corresponding prices leads to varying interpretations of demand (Haemmerle and Lehar 1987). Thus, different subsets of demand can be compared using benchmark index figures at 100 points. As a result, the so-called *parity index* can describe the relative price levels prevailing between the six accommodation categories by explicitely showing the marginal impact of a demand unit in different accommodation categories relative to the overall benchmarking result. Figure 5 again demonstrates for example the high "structural" importance of higher-standard accommodation units for the Tyrolean tourism industry as a whole.

FIGURE 5. Parity index.

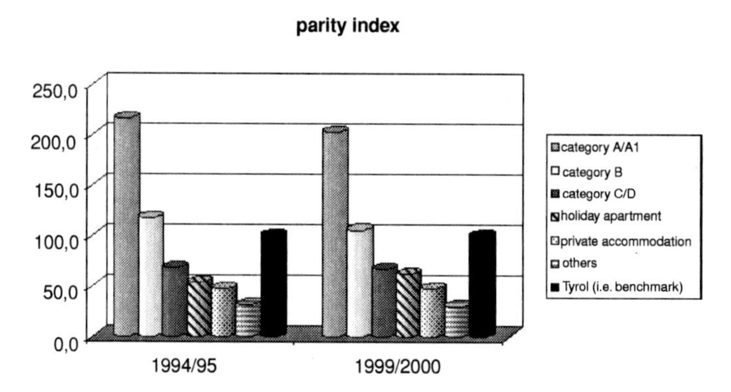

Source: kindly provided by Amt der Tiroler Landeregierung, Department of Statistics, 2001

Finally, the *destination type index* measures differences between the destination's price levels relative to the benchmark area on account of differing levels of attractiveness (e.g., site, tourism infrastructure) which are likely to be reflected also in prices of the accommodation sector (Haemmerle and Lehar 1987). The high relevance of the Tyrolean Capital-City tourism (destination type 1), the big price impact of tourism centres (destination type 2) and finally the relative price importance of all-season destinations (destination type 3) for the Tyrolean tourism industry can thus be also explained empirically (see Figure 6).

Lessons from the Case Study

After having thoroughly discussed both, the methodological as well as the empirical aspects of the *Tyrolean Tourism Barometer,* it should now be mentioned that this tool can not be used without reservations. Put differently, there could exist a number of theoretically deduced suggestions for its improvement. Let's consider first the main strengths of the tool. To successfully apply the *Tyrolean Tourism Barometer* only a relatively small amount of input data is necessary. Most secondary data are already available in the sense that the National Statistical Office already provides the necessary raw data. This, of course, results in relatively low costs for data collection and administration. Finally the tool fulfills the requirements of representativity, validity and reliability as it is able to quantify structural shifts in tourism supply and demand with regard to different regional areas.

FIGURE 6. Destination type index.

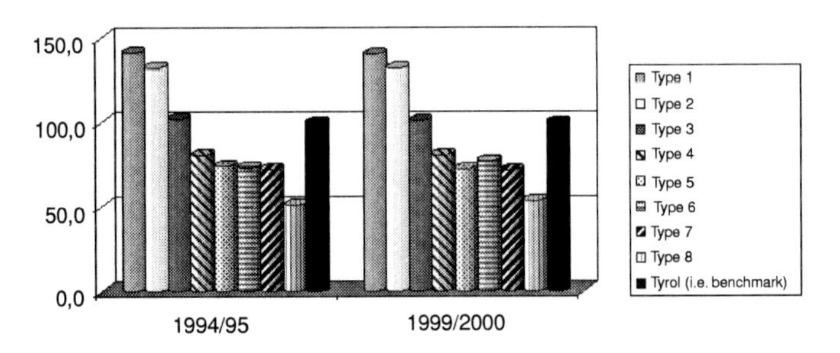

Source: kindly provided by Amt der Tiroler Landeregierung, Department of Statistics, 2001

The main weakness of the *Tyrolean Tourism Barometer* is not its conceptional simplicity or the fact that it only focuses at the accommodation industry. In order to establish a reliable instrument for retrospectively evaluating past tourism policy decisions and/or for optimizing future destination policies and strategies it will not be sufficient to only describe structural shifts in tourism supply and demand on the basis of *aggregated* quantitative data alone. For instance, by establishing various sub-market indicators, the barometer model could offer estimates also for structural shifts with regard to different *sending regions*. The most important critique is the entire neglect of the barometer with respect to highly relevant elements within the production process of tourism (i.e., destination) services. Thus, a vast enhancement of the tool's performance may only be realized by simultaneously considering all the major input resources needed to provide destination services, such as managerial and technical skills, investors' resources and the tourists' expectations on the demand side. In order to optimize service operations within tourism destinations, besides purely quantitative output measures (i.e., overnight stays) more complex output measures must be established. A highly important one would consist in the satisfaction level experienced by tourists during their composite value-adding process within destinations (Weiermair and Fuchs 1998, Kozak 2000). Up to now, very little research has been done to theoretically develop and empirically measure such complex efficiency measures which could also be used to optimize yield capacities as components of tourist destinations (Carú and Cugini 1998, Pullman and Moore 1998, Dall'Aglio 1999, Fuchs 2000).

In order to examine the role and difficulties of benchmarking approaches for tourist destinations, its most characterizing features must be stated systematically. Tourism services offered and produced in destinations are compounded by many elements. Laws (1995) identifies primary elements contributing to the attractiveness of a tourist destination as being climate, ecology, culture and traditional architecture and secondary elements being specifically designed for tourist groups, for example hotels, catering, transport activities and entertainment (Laws 1995, p. 36). Although primary features are consumed by tourists, the development of destinations primarily depends on the secondary (i.e., man-made) infrastructure. It follows, that tourism services are produced by many subsystems that jointly offer and deliver these services along one single destination service chain (Buhalis 2000). In economic language, subsystems within destinations combine a number of input resources in order to transform them to desired output levels. Thus, on the one hand benchmarking could focus on the performance of these many subsystems, but on the other hand different outcomes for tourism stakeholders (e.g., tourist satisfaction, work satisfaction, career development of staff, remuneration) may be worthwhile for benchmarking (Laws 1995, p. 37). Consequently, both, input resources as well as the economic output of these production and consumption processes within destinations should be considered simultaneously. Such an approach, of course, would lead to comprehensive and complex destination efficiency measures. Systems theory would argue that the efficiency of a destination's operation will be affected by changes on account of any of the elements of which it is composed (Laws 1995). For effective management which intends to control and optimize these processes a clear understanding of these effects on outputs of any change of its inputs and the ways in which internal subsystems and processes are linked is absolutely indispensable (Wöber 2000*a*). Thus, control over the quality and consistency of a destination's performance may also highly depend on effective feedback channels between these interdependent monitoring and decision-making subsystems (Zairi 1992).

CONCLUSIONS AND OUTLOOK

The above demonstrated barometer approach is defining quality in a purely technical and almost tautological manner by reducing it to shifts in turnover relative to its corresponding price developments. Although this barometer application may be justified as predominantely economically oriented, it should be pointed out that turnover measures represent neither the *profitability* nor the *efficiency* of tourism enterprises within a destination resort (Berktold 1992, p. 78). A more valuable support may be expected from periodical results obtained by the so called Travel and Tourism Satellite Accounts (*TTSA*'s) implemented among all the OECD member states in the near future (Okubo and

Planting 1998). The *TTSA*'s are particularly useful because tourism generally is not treated as a separate industry, so comprehensive value added data on tourism in most national economic statistics and accounting do not exist. Such data are instead scattered among other economic branches and sub-branches–for example transportation services, restaurants and sporting goods (Kass and Okubo 2000, p. 8). The *TTSA*'s are based on input output (*I-O*) accounts, which trace the full range of commodities and services that are produced by each industry and are used by final consumers (e.g., business and pleasure tourists, resident and nonresident tourists) and which also include the industry distributions of the value added. The latter is defined as the Tourism industry output (i.e., tourism domestic production) minus the required intermediate inputs including the compensation of employees. Up to now most *TTSA*'s are designed and implemented only on a nation-wide level and therefore do not permit reliable estimates of the tourism industry's value added at a provincial and/or resort (i.e., destination) level. Future tourism industry related monitoring systems should close this gap by adapting the *TSSA*'s approach at a provincial level to allow a more detailled evaluation of the value adding properties among different destinations and to roughly estimate returns on different resources used for the production of tourism services. By creating weighting schemes which enclose the level of resource consumption, such destination-specific information would enhance the validity of the benchmark indicators of the barometer model demonstrated above by detecting possible sub-optimal resource allocation conditions.

Further research has also to be done, to find out which combinations of quality dimensions and which quantities are perceived, experienced and/or consumed by tourists within each category of tourism facility (e.g., opening hours, accessibility to disabled or elderly guests, pricing policies, etc.). A highly valuable multivariate technique to benchmark operational efficiencies is the data envelopment analysis (Schefczyk and Gerpott 1995, Post and Spronk 1999). So far there exist some very interesting tourism benchmark studies which have attempted to employ this technique (Johns et al. 1997, Mayerhuber et al. 1998, Wöber 2000b). The method can be best described as a tool which has the ability to compare efficiencies of multiple service units that provide similar services by explicitly considering their use of multiple inputs to produce multiple outputs. The model attempts to maximize a service unit's efficiency, expressed as a ratio of outputs to inputs, by comparing a particular unit's efficiency with the performance of a benchmark (Fitzsimmons and Fitzsimmons 1997, p. 451). The experience with benchmarking in the context of a destination using a unidemensional and less developed tool, such as the *Tyrolean Tourism Barometer,* suggests that data envelopment analysis will probably play in the future a leading role in tourism-related benchmark applications.

REFERENCES

Amt der Tiroler Landesregierung (1987) *Typisierung der Tiroler Fremdenverkehrsgemeinden-Ergebnisse einer statistischen Analyse.* Amt der Tiroler Landesregierung/ Sachgebiet Statistik.

Berktold, E. (1992) *Qualitative Tourismusindikatoren.* Amt der Tiroler Landesregierung/ Sachgebiet Statistik.

Boger, C.A., L.A. Cai, and Li-C. Lin (1999) Benchmarking: Comparing discounted business rates among lodging companies. *Journal of Hospitality and Tourism Research*, 23(3), 256-267.

Bottomley, V. (1995) *Tourism: Competing with the Best.* Benchmarking for Smaller Hotels. KPMG study, London: Department of National Heritage.

Breiter, D. and S.F. Kline (1995) Benchmarking quality management in hotels. *FIU Hospitality Review*, 13(2), 45.

Buhalis, D. (2000) Marketing the competitive destination of the future. *Tourism Management* 21(1) 97-116.

Camp, R.C. (1995) *Business Process Benchmarking: Finding and Implementing Best Practices.* Milwaukee, WI: American Society for Quality Control Quality Press.

Carú, A. and A. Cugini (1998) *Profitability and customer satisfaction in services: an integrated perspective between marketing and cost management analysis.* In: Conference proceedings of the 5th International Research Seminar on Service Management, La Londe les Maures, France, 134-154.

Cook, S. (1995) *Practical Benchmarking: A Manager's Guide to creating a Competitive Advantage.* London: Kogan Page.

Dall'Aglio, S. (1999) *H.O.S.T. A Benchmarking System for the Hotel sector.* Paper presented at TRC meeting, Vienna

Dubé, L., C.A. End, L.M. Renaghan and J.A. Siguaw (1999) *American Lodging Excellence: The Key to Best Practice in the U.S. Lodging Industry.* Washington, DC: American Express and the American Hotel Foundation.

Everitt, B. (1980) *Cluster Analysis.* 2nd ed. New York: Halsted Press.

Fitzsimmons, J.A. and M. Fitzsimmons (1997) *Service Management-Operations, Strategy and Information Technology.* 2nd edition, Boston, IrwinMcGraw-Hill.

Fuchs, M. and K. Weiermair (1998) Qualitätsmessung vernetzter Dienstleistungen am Beispiel des alpinen Wintertourismus. *Tourismus Journal*, 2(2), 211-235.

Fuchs, M. (2000) Controlling als methodische Voraussetzung zur erfolgreichen Planung im Hotelbetrieb. *Journal of Tourism and Hospitality Management*, 5(1-2), 195-210.

Fuchs, M., L. Rijken, M. Peters and K. Weiermair (2000) Modelling Asian Incoming Tourism: A Shift-Share Approach. *Asia Pacific Journal of Tourism Research*, 5(2), 1-10.

Go, F. and R. Govers (2000) Integrated quality management for tourist destinations: a European perspective on achieving competitiveness. *Tourism Management*, 21(1), 79-88.

Haemmerle, W. and G. Lehar (1987) *Tiroler Tourismusbarometer*, Tiroler Fremdenverkehrswerbung.

Hair, J.F., R.E. Anderson, R.L. Tatham and W.C. Black (1995) *Mutltivariate Data Analysis*. Fourth ed. New Jersey: Prentice Hall.

Johns, N., D. Lee-Ross, R. Graves-Morris and H. Ingram (1996) *Quality benchmarking in the small hotel sector using profile accumulation: a new measurement tool.* In: Conference Proceedings of the 5th Annual Hospitality Research Conference, Nottingham Trent University, 192-207.

Johns, N., B. Howcroft and L. Drake (1997) The use of Data Envelopment Analysis to monitor hotel productivity. *Progress in Tourism and Hospitality Research*, 3(2), 119-127.

Karlof, B. and S. Ostblom (1994) *Benchamarking: A Signpost Excellence in Quality and Productivity*. West Sussex: John Wiley

Kass, David and S. Okubo (2000) U.S. Travel and Tourism Satellite Accounts for 1996 and 1997. *Survey of Current Business* (July):8-24.

Kaufman, H. and H. Pape (1984) *Clusteranalyse*. In: Fahrmeier, L. and Hamerle, A. (Eds.): Multivariate statistische Verfahren, Berlin-New York: Walter de Gruyter.

Kozak, M. (2000) *Destination Benchmarking: Facilities, Customer Satisfaction and Levels of Tourist Expenditure*. Ph.D.-Thesis, Sheffield Hallam University, UK.

Kozak, M. and M. Rimmington (1998) Benchmarking: destination attractiveness and small hospitality business performance. *International Journal of Contemporary Hospitality Management*, 10(5), 184-188.

Krug, W., M. Nourney and J. Schmidt (1994) *Wirtschafts-und Sozialstatistik-Gewinnung von Daten*, Wien, München: Oldenbourg.

Laws, E. (1995) *Tourist Destination Management*. Routledge, London.

Leibfried, K.H. and C.J. McNair (1992) *Benchmarking: A tool for continuous improvement*. New York, NY: Harper Business.

Mayrhuber, Chr., I. Paterson and A. Wörgötter (1998) *Arbeitsmarkt-und Beschäftigungssystem des Bundeslandes Tirol*. In: Weiermair, K. and M. Fuchs (Eds.) Conference proceedings RETTOURISM II, University of Innsbruck, Austria, 40-112.

McInyre, R.M. and R.K. Blashfield (1980) A Nearest-Centroid Technique for Evaluating the Minimum-Variance Clustering Procedure. *Multivariate Behavioural Research*, 15:225-238.

Morey, R.C. and D.A. Dittman (1995) Evaluating a hotel GM's performance. A case study in benchmarking. *Cornell Hotel and Restaurant Administration Quarterly*, 36(5), 30-35.

Murphy, P., M.P. Prichard and B. Smith (2000) The destination product and its impact on traveller perceptions. *Tourism Management*, 21(1), 43-52.

Post, T. and J. Spronk (1999) Performance benchmarking using interactive data envelopment analysis. *European Journal of Operations Research*, 115(3), 472-487.

Pullman, M.E. and W. Moore (1998) *Service Capacity Planning with Conjoint Analysis: Combining Marketing and Operations Perspectives for Profit Maximization.* In: Conference proceedings of the 5th International Research Seminar on Service Management, La Londe les Maures, France, 611-632.

Punj, G. and D. Stewart (1983) Cluster Analysis in Marketing Research: Review and Suggestions for Application. *Journal of Marketing Research*, 20(May):134-148.

Ritchie, B.J.R. and G.I. Crouch (2000) The competitive destination. A sustainable perspective. *Tourism Management*, 21(1), 1-7.

Schefczyk, M. and T.J. Gerpott (1995) Ein produktionswirtschaftlicher Benchmarking-Ansatz: Data Envelopment Analysis. *Journal für Betriebswirtschaft*, 5(6), 335-346.

Siguaw, J.A. and C.A. Enz (1999a) Best practices in food and beverage management. *Cornell Hotel and Restaurant Administration Quarterly*, 40(5), 50-57.

Siguaw, J.A. and C.A. Enz (1999b) Best practices in hotel operations. *Cornell Hotel and Restaurant Administration Quarterly*, 40(6), 42-53.

Siguaw, J.A. and C.A. Enz (1999c) Best practices in marketing. *Cornell Hotel and Restaurant Administration Quarterly*, 40(5), 31-43.

Sinclair, M.Th. and M. Stabler (1997) *The Economics of Tourism*. New York, NY: Routhledge.

Sirakaya, E., M. Uysal and L. Toepper (1995) Measuring tourism performance using a shift-share analysis: The case of South Carolina. *Journal of Travel Research*, 34(2), 55-61

Smith, G.A, D. Ritter and W.P Tuggle (1993) Benchmarking: the fundamental questions. *Marketing Management*, 2(3), 43-48.

Spendolini, M.J. (1992) *The Benchmarking Book*. New York, NY: Amacom.

Sumiye, Okubo and M.A. Planting (1998) U.S. Travel and Tourism Satellite Accounts for 1992. *Survey of Current Business* (July): 8-22.

Tschurtschenthaler, P. (1998) *Humankapitalentwicklung als tourismuspolitisches Instrument zur Bewältigung der Tourismuskrise*. In: Weiermair, K. and M. Fuchs (Eds.) Conference proceedings RETTOURISM II, University of Innsbruck, 16-39.

Weiermair, K. and M. Fuchs (1998) *Quality Dimensions in Alpine Tourism and their Assessment by Tourists and Tourism Entrepreneurs*. In: Conference proceedings of the 5th International Research Seminar on Service Management, La Londe les Maures, France, 840-859.

Weiermair, K. and M. Fuchs (1999) Measuring Tourist Judgments on Service Quality. *Annals of Tourism Research*, 26(4), 1004-1021.

Wöber, K. (2000a) *Efficiency measures in benchmarking decision support systems. A hotel industry application*. In: Buhalis, D. and D. Fesenmaier (Eds.) Information and Communication Technologies in Tourism. Wien: Springer (forthcoming).

Wöber, K. (2000b) *Optimal Selection of Comparison Partners for Business Performance Studies. A Lodging Industry Experimental Study*. Post-doctoral Thesis, University of Vienna, Austria (unpublished).

Zairi, M. (1992) The art of benchmarking: using customer feedback to establish a performance gap. *Total Quality Management*, 3(2), 177-188.

Zairi, M. (1996) *Benchmarking for Best Practice: Continuous Learning Through Sustainable Innovation*. Oxford: Butterworth-Heinemann.

Benchmarking Best Practice in Hotel Front Office: The Western European Experience

Tom Baum
Peter Odgers

SUMMARY. During the past decade there have been significant changes in the hotel sector, the marketplace and its operations. This paper reports a research study across a number of western European countries into the changing functions within front office operations and the role of personnel in a range of hotels and locations. Issues addressed include the flattening of organisations; the increasing expectation of multi-tasking and multi-skilling; and creating a balance between technological solutions and the delivery of quality customer care. These issues are linked to wider findings on the growth in the need for the more generic skill types together with the importance of personal attributes as key selection criteria and the growing emphasis of the employers role in providing training for vocational skills. Work in these areas has seen a decline in routine activities and has become increasingly complex, involving the use of a wide range of software, maintaining in-house systems and the expectations of faster response to more complex methods of communications. Industry has realised the importance of customer care

Tom Baum is affiliated with the University of Strathclyde, Curran Building, 43, Cathedral Street, Glasgow G4 0LG (E-mail: t.g.baum@strath.ac.uk).

Peter Odgers is affiliated with the University of Brighton, 49 Darley Road, Eastbourne, East Sussex BN20 7UR (E-mail: p.odgers@bton.ac.uk).

[Haworth co-indexing entry note]: "Benchmarking Best Practice in Hotel Front Office: The Western European Experience." Baum, Tom, and Peter Odgers. Co-published simultaneously in *Journal of Quality Assurance in Hospitality & Tourism* (The Haworth Hospitality Press, an imprint of The Haworth Press, Inc.) Vol. 2, No. 3/4, 2001, pp. 93-109; and: *Benchmarks in Hospitality and Tourism* (ed: Sungsoo Pyo) The Haworth Hospitality Press, an imprint of The Haworth Press, Inc., 2001, pp. 93-109. Single or multiple copies of this article are available for a fee from The Haworth Document Delivery Service [1-800-HAWORTH, 9:00 a.m. - 5:00 p.m. (EST). E-mail address: getinfo@haworthpressinc.com].

and the subsequent increase in focus by operators on its provision. These issues have led to the setting of procedures and benchmarks for the various functions and services of front office and the empowerment of employees in their implementation. The paper provides an insight into changes in front office and the manner in which technology is acting as an enabling force rather than replacing traditional roles. The paper addresses education and training implications for the hotel sector and education providers by examining current curricula and training provision and questions the relevance of some "sacred cows" that have traditionally been taught. The paper concludes with recommendations for future education and training provision.

KEYWORDS. Benchmarking, personnel selection criteria, training, front office, technology

INTRODUCTION

During the past decade the hotel sector has evolved and developed in organisational, product and market terms with significant consequences for the nature of work in hospitality organisations. The changes in the hotel sector have in the main been due to the growth of multiple ownership, the globalisation and stronger branding of hotel chains (Go and Pine, 1995; Guerrier et al., 1998).

The changing profile and dynamics of English tourism featuring new trends and tourism patterns over the past decade has led to the marketplace experiencing increased occupancy rates and hotel usage (ETC, 2001). These changing patterns of customer activity have been influenced by changes in their traditional profiles and show them to be more knowledgeable, more product aware and demanding better value for money (Henley Centre, 1996). Industry operators have responded to this through an increased focus on the provision of customer service and benchmarking its products and services (BHA/Scher, 2000).

Hotel operations during this period have also seen significant changes in the role and influence of technology (Henley Centre/JHIC, 1996) with the growing use of more sophisticated communications and integrated administration packages from specialist providers. All hotels surveyed in the study reported in this paper used computer technology to a greater or lesser extent for routine functions such as billing, reservations and correspondence while the majority either operated or were developing their own web site. Burgess (2000) in a survey of hotel financial managers found that the influence of 'high tech' approaches to front office operating systems had also enhanced the role of 'high touch' in increased personal service and that these impacts had lead to higher guest expectations. As a contrast to research, a study into the use of technology by tourism and hospitality operators in Wales (Jones et al., 1999) showed that many micro hospitality businesses have IT equipment but there is a low level of exploitation for business purposes.

The hospitality industry draws its workforce, in developed societies, from a predominantly youth labour market, both at skilled and unskilled levels. This is, in part, a reflection of the recent growth of the sector but is also a consequence of other factors, notably the variable demand cycle within hospitality reflected in seasonality; the physical requirements of work in the industry; its demanding conditions; and the status of hospitality as a transitory rather than permanent career option. It is also a reflection of a demand in the industry for what Warhurst et al. (2000) call "aesthetic labour", employees whose physical, educational and social characteristics are similar to those of consumers–this is by no means new in the airline sector, for example, but is of increasing importance in other areas of hospitality, not least the hotel front desk.

Warhurst et al. identify that this trend is by no means universal and is of particular relevance to urban businesses, boutique hotels, style bars and theme restaurants, where the use of "aesthetic" criteria in employment may outweigh conventional skills and knowledge considerations. Such trends have profound significance for an industry which recruits in a labour market that is increasingly constrained. Front office work demands relatively high educational and social skills levels and competes for labour with a range of professional and para-professional areas of work, notably those identified by BBC Careers (2000) to include all types of administrative-related work both generic and specific. There is also evidence of a merging of traditional functions and increasing cross-functional collaboration, the upskilling effects in many jobs and new and broader mixes of skills including skill combinations within occupations (multi-skilling); across functions; across occupational groups (hybridisation); and across skill/occupation/academic levels.

Within a constrained labour market, ensuring access to opportunity for a growing proportion of the population is critical. In the case of potential entrants to careers in hospitality front office, the key groups under-represented in education generally and/or work in this sector specifically include those from poorer economic backgrounds; those from rural areas; and males.

Issues raised by this research are linked to wider findings on the growth in the need for the more generic skill types together with the importance of personal attributes as key selection criteria and the growing emphasis of the employer's role in providing training for vocational skills (National Skills Task Force, 2000). Perhaps the work environment most closely allied to hotel front office is that of generic office work and changes in this context have been effectively identified in a recent Canadian study (Human Resource Development Canada, 1999). This study shows the changing functions in many areas of work, including office administration. Work in these areas has seen a decline in routine activities and is increasingly complex, involving the use of a wide range of software, coordinating data entry and maintaining in-house systems, analysing and understanding data for trends and anomalies and the expectations of faster response to more complex methods of communications whilst working for a variety of client companies at the same time. This Canadian study goes on to identify the areas of office work such as the various accounting, inventory control and clerical functions that are most vulnerable to changes in work practice. The study also identifies those areas that are most likely to benefit from such changes by focusing on the provision of customer service, the co-ordination and scheduling of workplace activities, managing data processing and the range of communication functions. These provide indications of change within allied work areas such as front office. The challenge for office workers and their employers, identified by the HRD Canada study, suggests an agenda for lifelong learning in this area of employment and provides valuable indicators when determining curriculum focus that can be translated in terms of front office work.

The generic skills debate is supported by the *HtF Hospitality Sector Workforce Development Plan for 2001* (HtF, 2000) reporting that in terms of skills gaps among staff, employers indicate that principally it is generic skills that need to be improved in the workforce. The report identifies these skills as being communications, showing initiative, delivering customer service and showing a willingness to learn.

Industry has realised the importance of customer care and there has been a subsequent increase in focus by operators on its provision. These issues have led to the setting of standard procedures and benchmarks for the various functions and services of front office and the empowerment of employees in their implementation.

RESEARCH OBJECTIVES

This study was undertaken between September and December 2000 on behalf of CERT, Ireland with the objective of benchmarking best practice in front office provision as part of their ongoing curriculum review process for their course programmes and institutions in Ireland. Within this context, this paper reports a research study across a number of Western European countries that have hospitality sectors comparable to that in the Irish Republic into the changing functions within front office operations in a range of hotels and locations and into the changing role of front office personnel.

Issues addressed by the research include the operational effects of the flattening of the organisation in front office; the increasing expectation of multi-tasking and multi-skilling; and creating a balance between technological solutions and the delivery of quality customer care.

METHODOLOGY

The initial step within this study was to undertake a comprehensive search of secondary resources that could usefully inform the fieldwork element of the research. This was undertaken through a diversity of strategies including formal literature searches, posted requests for assistance on various hospitality and tourism e-networks, direct contact with relevant hospitality, training and educational organizations and communications with individuals and companies with an identified interest in the area. The outcome of the secondary source review process was a rapidly reached conclusion that no "off-the-shelf" model and answer to the research brief was available internationally and, indeed, that the area was one that has suffered neglect and had only limited consideration by academics and practitioners.

The primary research consisted of semi-structured interviews with front office personnel at operational, supervisory and management levels in site visits to 80 hotels across the range of hotel types, sizes and locations. Of this sample half were independently owned operations and the interviews were held in resort, urban and city locations in hotels in England, France, Germany, Ireland, Scotland, Spain, Sweden, and Switzerland. Focus group meetings involving owners, managers, front office operatives, teachers and past and current students were also held in England, France, Ireland, Sweden and Germany.

BENCHMARKING

The process of benchmarking provides the basis for identifying best practice in the area of front office operations, management and training with a particular focus on likely future trends and developments. Benchmarking may be defined as *the search for industry best practice that will lead to superior performance* (Camp, 1989; Longbottom, 2000).

In undertaking a benchmarking exercise, it is necessary to identify the range of criteria against which performance will be measured. The selected criteria must reflect the business characteristics of the sector or activity in question in terms of factors such as unit size; business type; and location. Of particular importance to this study is the need to recognise dependencies so that the benchmarking exercise cannot be viewed in isolation. This is recognised in our consideration of the wider context in this review.

Useful criteria for benchmarking are provided by Mann et al. (1999) in the context of the food and drinks industry. Their indicative examples of criteria include:

- leadership
- policy and strategy
- people management
- resource management
- process management
- customer satisfaction
- people satisfaction
- impact on society/community
- business results

These criteria can be translated into terms and conditions that are applicable to the front office area of hotels.

- management/supervisory culture (empowerment?)
- links between core areas (reservations, customer care, finance, MI)
- people management (links to culture)
- resource utilisation (IT, e-business)
- customer handling/satisfaction
- impact on community
- business results

DEFINING BENCHMARKING AND BEST PRACTICE FOR THE HOTEL FRONT OFFICE

Benchmarking and Best practice, in relation to hotel Front Office, are difficult terms to define, in part because of the diversity that exists within the industry. It is not appropriate or possible to identify singular best practice or benchmarking standards that are universally applicable across the hotel sector in Western Europe or elsewhere. The hotel Front Office must measure its practices in the light of the specific context of the operation within which it is located and in a manner that is appropriate to its market and business requirements. While Rose's concept of *Lesson Drawing* (Rose, 1992) is applicable to the transfer of good ideas and good practice from one hotel context to another, such adoption cannot be undertaken in an uncritical manner. Best practice definitions accord closely to that of lesson drawing but tend to focus on the specifics of one area of an activity rather than adopting Rose's more holistic approach that looks at the whole business operation in context. Both approaches have value in allowing one business to develop on the basis of the experiences of others and in the framing of educational and training programmes.

The US Lodging Report (1999) defines Best Practice as "any practice, know-how, or experience that has proven to be valuable or effective within one organisation that may have applicability to other organisations." Benchmarking, a related concept, involves the measurement of the performance of one operation or business (or part thereof) against the specific performance of another, directly comparable operation or against the performance of the comparable sector as a whole. Benchmarking provides the means by which performance can be measured in specific areas and best practice identified.

Benchmarks of performance can be readily used within standardised hotel front office operations. Central reservations functions, for example, establish benchmarks against which telephone queries are timed and managed. Similar criteria can be established for in-house reservation queries where many of the likely questions can be predicted and responses planned–a fixed price policy, for example, removes much area for discussion and allows "norms" to be set for both personal and telephone enquiries about availability.

The British Hospitality Association (BHA) in liaison with Scher consultancy is carrying out on an ongoing basis research into guest satisfaction with hotel services, some of which focus on front office provision. A number of functions in the front office operation have been benchmarked through measuring efficiency on a timed response basis against those functions which are measured against the human aspect of delivery. The research has measured customer satisfaction with these criteria across the range of hotel provision with the outcome that the more labour intensive luxury operation give a significantly higher degree of satisfaction than mid market and budget operations. In this study, benchmarks were identified to cover some but not all front office activities. These were processes of a more routine and less individualised nature, including those set out in Table 1.

Similar process benchmarks are less readily set in the front office of a hotel that offers diversity in its product and places an emphasis on personal attention for its guests. Here, best practice, in the form of the lessons that can be drawn from the experience of other, similar properties may be much more valuable.

TABLE 1. Sample Process Benchmarks for Hotel Front Office

PROCESS	BENCHMARK
Enquiry	Response times–telephone; post; e-mail–as agreed
Reservations	Response times as agreed
Check-in	Timed procedures as agreed
In-house–administrative	Standard house procedures and presentation
In-house–accounting and billing	100% accurate
Handling guests–general	Standard house procedures
Handling guests–selling opportunities	Successful sale
Check-out	Timed procedures as agreed
Room release for servicing	Within agreed response time after check-out
Guest follow-up	Standard house procedures
Systems training	New staff member competent and confident within prescribed time

Benchmarks can also be established against external criteria, either within the group or against more general, industry performance averages for the type of property in the location, region or country. Some of these benchmarks may not be readily available. Table 2 provides a sample of such benchmarks for the front office area.

IDENTIFYING BEST PRACTICE IN HOTEL FRONT OFFICE

This study identified a number of best practice case examples relating to a variety of different areas of hotel front office operations, work and training. The case examples illustrated here are by no means exhaustive but illustrate the response of various stakeholders to the changing environment of hotel front office. Table 3 gives a selection of best practice mini cases.

KEY FINDINGS

Perhaps the most significant finding from this study was that, fundamentally, job categories in front office have not changed significantly in recent years although there appears to have been a decline in the position of *Assistant*

TABLE 2. Sample External Benchmarks for Hotel Front Office

AREA OF ACTIVITY	BENCHMARK
Annual Occupancy %	5% above group or city average
Weekend occupancy	Within 10% of city average
Revpar	Group/ city average
Repeat business	Group/city average
Written complaints	10% below group average
Non-resident F & B sales	10% above city average ratio
Enquiry conversions	Group/city average

TABLE 3. Mini Case Studies of Front Office Best Practice

ORGANISATION/ CONTEXT	CASE EXAMPLE
London Hilton	Customer Service Operative model for multi-skilling between Front Office and Service. Substantial pay rise for staff once fully multi-skilled.
Jurys Inns, Ireland & UK	Expectation by all Front Office staff of coverage in other departments when required.
Scandic Hotels, Ibis, Mercure Hotels	Combined Front Office and Café/ Bar facility in smaller hotels, operated seamlessly by Front Office staff.
Scandic Hotels	"Sigge Skole" induction programme on intranet for all new employees with 8 hours required study at commencement of employment–ensures IT literacy of all staff. Critically, Sigge Skole also recognises the need for all new staff to gain a holistic view of the operation.
Scandic Hotels	All Front Office staff have access to own e-mail account and to staff intranet for company information and job vacancies.
Jurys Hotels	Normal practice for Front Office Managers and promoted Front Office staff to be internal promotion appointees–creation of real career opportunities in Front Office.
Jurys Hotel, Bristol	£10 placed in Front Office kitty for each nights's 100% occupancy achieved
Marriott Hotels	Focused Front Office staff training on first ten minutes of guest stay as the "make or break" period for customer satisfaction.
Marriott Hotels	Each day, Front Office staff are issued with a prompt card which focuses on main points relevant to a particular element of customer service.

or *Junior Receptionist*. This is particular to hotels in major cities and as a response to problems in filling such positions. Given the virtual elimination of traditional, routine office-related tasks such as basic typing, filing and photocopying, it is, in any case, difficult to distinguish between the job content of *Junior Receptionist* and *Receptionist*. Therefore, this study does not recognise the former as a separate job category. Rather, a distinction is made between the role of receptionist in the small and large hotel.

The following staff categories were identified as common across the survey hotels in the countries included in the study:

- Receptionist–small/medium-sized independently-owned hotel
- Receptionist–medium/large-sized chain-owned hotel
- Head Receptionist/Front Office Manager-small/medium-sized independently owned hotel
- Shift Leader/Head Receptionist–Large hotel–independent or chain-operated
- Front Office Manager–Large Hotel–independent or chain-operated
- Reservations Manager–Large Hotel–independent or chain-operated
- Revenue Manager–Large Chain-Operated Hotel

Job categories may not have altered greatly in recent years but the emphasis within each job has undoubtedly broadened. In general, changes of emphasis identified include

- *Jobs more knowledge based rather than technical based*: This applies to all categories of front office staff. The technical demands of the job have reduced with the advent of efficient and easy-to-use systems. Customers demand more detailed and accurate information about the hotel and its environs and expect solutions to their problems in a timely and accurate manner.
- *Expanded supervisory and management role*: Management and supervisory functions have expanded through greater delegation/empowerment and the elimination of intermediate management positions.
- *Multi-skilling*: The virtual elimination of set roles within front office requires all staff to contribute to all aspects of the front office function, frequently extending to areas such as reservations, concierge and telephonist. Most small hotels and many budget hotel groups expect multi-skilling to extend to aspects of food and beverage service.
- *A holistic view of the hotel and its services*: In many instances, the hotel business has become much more revenue conscious relative to all areas

of activity and the front office is required to up-sell the full range of in-house services, some of which may be externally contracted.

- *Understanding guest needs at an individual level*: Customers are increasingly demanding and expect tailored responses to their particular requirements. Front office is the natural port of call with these queries and staff require quality communication and information searching skills.
- *Greater emphasis on the provision of on-the-job training*: With current high turnover rates in the European hotel industry and the difficulty in recruiting qualified and experienced staff, the provision of on-going, on-the-job training by experienced staff is essential to maintain service standards.
- *Changing approach to front office staff recruitment*: In the absence of experienced, qualified staff, many hotels increasingly look to generic, non-technical competencies (communication, problem solving, customer service and IT) in recruiting new personnel and build in extended on-the-job-training within the induction phase.
- *Planned training and career development*: Front office departments provide an excellent environment for planned career development of staff and succession planning. This requires a commitment to on-going training and development (in-house and external) in order to prepare staff for new responsibilities. Within larger organisations surveyed, internal promotion structures from receptionist through to management positions in areas such as reservations and revenue were well defined and supported.
- With some exceptions automation and the impact of technical change has simplified the role of front office but has not eliminated it. Front office personnel play no role in the development of creative IT solutions (web design etc.) and have greatly benefited from the simplification in the use of integrated hotel systems.
- Educational provision for front office has substantially failed to keep pace with changes in the industry environment and remains routed in an outmoded emphasis on technical competence development.

IMPLICATIONS OF STUDY FINDINGS FOR TRAINING NEEDS

The purpose of this study was to interpret changes in front office work in terms of what they mean for the provision of training in this area, both pre-entry and through continuous professional development (CPD). The implications for training are set out below.

THE HOTEL SECTOR

- *Growing influence of chain and franchise operations*: the influence of hotel product and service standardisation has contributed to a deskilling of some aspects of front office work, especially in the mid-and budget sectors of the market. The corollary of this is more widespread use of standard company training programmes for front office, enhancing the overall quality of in-house training.
- *Automation of systems and functions* will continue in European hotels but is unlikely to lead to a general automation of services at the expense of traditional front office roles.
- *Electronic marketing and reservations is increasing* with front office staff being required to service the outcomes in a timely and accurate manner. However, they have a very limited role in the development and management of such systems.
- *Yield management is operated to good effect within hotel management systems or via GDS* although decision-making by front office staff within these systems is limited. Understanding of the general principles of yield management, therefore, is important while detailed technical understanding is not required.

RECRUITMENT

- *Competitive labour markets*: hotels are competing for front office staff in highly competitive labour markets and must match opportunities for advancement, CPD and remuneration offered by other service sector employers and the IT sector.
- *Rural migration*: rural hotels face the challenge of youth migration towards urban centres, especially among young women, the traditional source of recruitment for front office.
- *The gender balance*: it is a particular challenge to attract young men into front office work and considerable restructuring of training, conditions and opportunities may be required to alter this.
- *Decline of office-type work*: Traditional sources of front office recruitment from secretarial and commercial colleges has declined because of the changing job content of front office work from administrative to customer-focused tasks.
- *Management internships in front office* are highly successful in the United States and elsewhere. Colleges and the industry could undertake

far more to promote this path to a career in front office for Diploma and Degree level students as an alternative to traditional food and beverage routes.

- *Non-traditional recruitment* from mature career changers and those returning to work provide opportunities that hotel companies appear to be willing to exploit in their international recruitment but have not fully addressed in terms of their local labour markets.

JOB CONTENT

- *Integration of skills requirements within the front office area*: job demarcation between the different areas of front office have all but disappeared and staff are expected to operate with confidence in all customer contact and many back-of-house areas.
- *Creating opportunity out of multi-skilling*: multi-skilling between front office and other areas of hotel work can no longer be seen as an inevitable but regrettable aspect of work in smaller hotels. Industry and training providers need to review the approaches of companies such as Hilton, Jurys Inn and Scandic by multi-skilling is a recognised route to career advancement.
- *Integration of technical and interpersonal skills in all aspects of work*: technical and interpersonal activities can no longer be seen independently but must be seen as complementary in meeting common business and guest satisfaction objectives.
- *Limited opportunities for specialist skills*: emerging skills requirements in IT (internet, web-design) are and will continue to be outsourced by hotels, providing little by way of job enrichment for Front Office staff.

EDUCATION AND TRAINING

- *The generic skills debate*: most employers in hospitality and related service sectors appear to place greatest emphasis on the development of a range of core generic skills within the training process and play down the value of technical, job specific competencies.
- *IT ready*: Employers and training providers have an expectation of education that school leavers should develop core IT skills and familiarity with general office and internet software prior to entering the training and employment market.

- *Language training* for front office staff is given low priority by the industry in English speaking countries and perhaps should be given a lower priority if this is "politically" acceptable.
- *Greater exposure to the workplace during training*: classroom theory and simulated role play is not an adequate substitution for exposure to the real workplace context. Early exposure to the industry increases confidence, competence, employability and commitment.
- *Developing professional interpersonal skills*: the need within the job to focus on generic, interpersonal and communication skills requires new and innovative approaches to teaching and learning and a consequent move away from traditional, knowledge-based approaches that focus on redundant technical skills development.
- *Front Office–a management apprenticeship*: Front office can no longer be seen as a craft area of hospitality work but as a grounding for career development into management and both the curriculum and context of programmes needs to reflect this.

CAREER DEVELOPMENT

- *Educational opportunity with an eye to further development*: progression opportunities are a key factor in influencing educational choice among young people and a lack of clear progression pathways from initial front office training is a clear weakness in smaller organisations.
- *Creating career development opportunities in front office*: changes in recruitment patterns and recognition of the value of in-house advancement has created clear career paths from front office to revenue and reservations management (in either sequence). These paths would benefit if reinforced through enhanced advanced training opportunities.
- *Developing the front office route to general management*: the increasing rooms focus of many hotel types places front office in a pivotal role in the hotel and provides opportunities for advancement to general management for those working in this area. Such moves require support through specialist training.

THE FOCUS OF FRONT OFFICE WORK IN THE NEXT DECADE

Notwithstanding evident and on-going changes to the consumer, hotel and labour markets, the over-riding conclusion from this study is that the "fundamentals" of hotel front office work will remain customer focused. Technology has and continues to develop to support the efficient delivery of quality service and to ease pressure on tight employment markets. It will not, however, radically change the core work of front office staff nor will it substitute for this work other than in exceptional cases within the economy sector of the market.

A key, evolving change in front office work is the integration of technical and interpersonal skills in all aspects of work. This is the result of growing emphasis on the latter while technology has developed as a support for the delivery of service rather than as an objective in itself. In a technical sense, technology will continue to reduce the skills demands of front office work as systems become more user friendly and share their basic operating features with widely used office and domestic computer software.

The role of the front office as an internal and external communications hub for the hotel will be enhanced and will require considerably greater skills on the part of staff at all levels. Internally, front office will continue to provide a focal point for all guest communications, with other departments and the external environment. Front office also acts *in loco* of management in providing the first line to handle indications of customer satisfaction, both positive and negative.

Within the hotel as a business, the integration of all systems places front office in the role of supporting back office activities relating to management information, financial information and yield management and requires staff in front office to evaluate and act upon such information as and when required. Front office also provides an essential communications link between each of the operating departments and ensures co-ordination in guest services provision between them. This role takes on added importance particularly where separate departments are either outsourced or contracted externally to a third party provider.

Externally, front office can provide links to a variety of allied organisations. It is an important conduit of two-way information between the hotel and its partner hotels within the group or associate hotels within a marketing consortium. Front office and/or reservations frequently manages links to GDS suppliers both manually and by electronic means. This link will grow in importance.

Within tight labour markets and in the absence of line management, front office staff are likely to face a growing requirement to handle key business decisions, especially relating to the management of yield and revenue and dealing with both positive and negative aspects of guest satisfaction.

Language skills, which are deemed essential in the recruitment of front office staff in many other European countries are unlikely to feature as a priority in the UK and Irish industry in the future. While the German and Swedish industries, for example, will not recruit staff without a second major European language, generally English, the perception in the UK and Ireland is that the vast majority of visitors to this country come in the expectation of using English and have reasonable competence in the language. Further language training, while perhaps desirable, is probably an unrealistic expectation and is one that college-based programmes are unlikely to undertake with any degree of success.

CONCLUSION

In conclusion, therefore, this study points to a Front Office area of increasing importance in the modern hotel, controlling the activities of other operational areas; liaising between various internal service providers; acting as the main guest interface point and playing a leading role in revenue generation. The hotel front office has not and will not become a high "tec" "nurd" centre, devoid of human interaction and staffed by IT specialists. With declining staff numbers and organisational flattening through the hotel, however, front office is clearly a nerve centre that demands further research into organisational, financial and customer service activities. Educational and training providers, in turn, will need to be sensitive to the front office work focus identified by this research.

REFERENCES

BBC (2000) *Career Moves–Office work* http://www.bbc.co.uk/education/lzone/newbusiness/caoffice.htm

BHA/Scher (2000) *Benchmark UK Industry Report*; London: BHA.

Burgess, C. (2000) "The hotel financial manager-challenges for the future." *International Journal of Contemporary Hospitality Management*, Vol.12, Issue 1.

Camp, R.C. (1995), *Business Process Benchmarking: Finding and Implementing Best Practice* Milwaukee: ASQC Quality Press

Canadian Tourism Human Resource Council.(1999*) National Occupational Standards for the Canadian Tourism Industry: Front Desk Agent.* Ottowa: CTHRC.

Department for Education and Employment (2000). *Skills for all: Research report from the National Skills Task Force*. London: DEE.

English Tourism Council (2001). *Perspectives of English Tourism.* London: ETC.

Go, F.H. and Pine, R. (1995) *Globalisation Strategy in the Hotel Industry*, New York: Routledge

Guerrier, Y, Baum,T, Jones, P and Roper,A. (1998) *In the World of Hospitality . . . anything they can do, we can do better*, London: JHIC/CHME.

Henley Centre/Joint Hospitality Industry Congress (1996) *Hospitality into the 21st Century-A vision for the future* London: JHIC.

Hospitality Training Foundation (2000) *Hospitality Sector Workforce Development Plan 2001 (Draft)*, London: HtF.

Jones. E., Dainty, G. And Botterill, D. (1999) *Use of Technology by Tourism Operators in Wales-Interim Report*, Cardiff: Wales Tourism Training Forum.

Longbottom, D. (2000) "Benchmarking in the UK: an empirical study of practicioners and academics" *Benchmarking: an International Journal*. Vol.7, Issue 2.

Mann, R; Adebanjo, O; and Kehoe, D. (1999) "Best practices in the food and drink industry" *British Food Journal* Vol.101, Issue 3.

Rose, R. (1993*) Lesson Drawing in Public Policy–A Guide to Learning Across Time and Space*. New Jersey: Chatham.

Warhurst, C., Nickson, D.,Witz, A. and Cullen, A.M.(2000) Aesthetic Labour in Interactive Service Work: Some Case Study Evidence from the 'New' Glasgow. *Service Industries Journal*, Vol.20, No.3 pp.1-18.

Managing Quality in Hotel Excelsior

Vesna Vrtiprah

SUMMARY. There is no doubt that quality in the hotel industry is an important issue. Delivering quality in hospitality operations involves reliably providing accommodation, food, service and entertainment within an environment that meets the expectations of customers, simultaneously creating opportunities for adding value that will exceed expectations and result in delight and repeat purchases or recommendations. Managing quality in hospitality operations is difficult, complicated by the complex blend of production and service elements that need to be managed over the short cycle of operations.

Hotel Excelsior initiated a benchmarking exercise in 5-star hotels and recognizing the contribution that quality might play in achieving company objectives in marketing and profitability, decided to gain ISO 9002 registration in July of 1999. ISO 9002 does not guarantee improvements in quality, but the management of Hotel Excelsior believes that the systems and controls have this effect. Hotel Excelsior has taken on that challenge. The paper analyzes how they established HRN EN ISO 9002 (Croatian Norm European Norm ISO 9002) and the advantages of an orientation towards quality. *[Article copies available for a fee from The Haworth Document Delivery Service: 1-800-HAWORTH. E-mail address: <getinfo@haworthpressinc.com> Website: <http://www.HaworthPress.com> © 2001 by The Haworth Press, Inc. All rights reserved.]*

KEYWORDS. Hotel industry, managing quality, ISO 9002, Hotel Excelsior, benefits

---

Vesna Vrtiprah is on the Faculty of Tourism and Foreign Trade, Lapadska obala 7, 20 000 Dubrovnik, Croatia (E-mail: bvesna@ftvt.hr).

[Haworth co-indexing entry note]: "Managing Quality in Hotel Excelsior." Vrtiprah, Vesna. Co-published simultaneously in *Journal of Quality Assurance in Hospitality & Tourism* (The Haworth Hospitality Press, an imprint of The Haworth Press, Inc.) Vol. 2, No. 3/4, 2001, pp. 111-126; and: *Benchmarks in Hospitality and Tourism* (ed: Sungsoo Pyo) The Haworth Hospitality Press, an imprint of The Haworth Press, Inc., 2001, pp. 111-126. Single or multiple copies of this article are available for a fee from The Haworth Document Delivery Service [1-800-HAWORTH, 9:00 a.m. - 5:00 p.m. (EST). E-mail address: getinfo@haworthpressinc.com].

INTRODUCTION

Many organizations use quality in the advertisements directed towards their customers and in the standards of performance manuals directed towards their staff. Product, service and process improvements can take place only in relation to established standards, after which the improvements are then incorporated into the new standards. Hotel Excelsior in Dubrovnik, exploring different approaches to quality and the benchmarking exercise in 5-star hotels, decided to gain ISO 9002 registration. The links between benchmarking and TQM are clear–establishing objectives based on industry best practice should directly contribute to the better meeting of internal and external customer requirements.

QUALITY DESIGN IN THE HOTEL INDUSTRY

Greater competition and with this the number of services on the tourist market gives the customer a strong position and the possibility of a wider range of services. Customers are well-informed and try to optimize their satisfaction, taking into consideration the time and money they have invested. They direct themselves towards hotels that offer the best quality, and they turn to other hotels if the quality does not match their expectations. This is the reason why service quality management was focused upon and particularly researched and used at the end of the seventies and at the beginning of the eighties. Quality is an important factor in the purchase decision and can help to avoid price competition and to maximize potential revenue.

Customers evaluate delivered service against their expectations. Expectations are formed by prior experience with the product, word-of-mouth, the firm's external communication, and publicity. High quality builds loyal customers and creates positive word-of-mouth. For this reason, the driving force of the quality management approach lies in focusing on the satisfaction of customer needs. This involves the whole organization in looking for ways of continually improving the products or services delivered.

Managing quality in hospitality operations is difficult, complicated by the complex blend of production and service elements that need to be managed over the short cycle of operations. Managing service quality has its own particularities that stem from the specific characteristics of services. Four points characterize service (Knowles, 1994: 32):

- services are intangible
- services are activities (performances) rather than things
- services are produced and consumed simultaneously
- the consumer participates in the production process to some extent.

Service quality is more difficult for the customer to evaluate than goods quality. Service quality perception results from a comparison of customer expectations with the actual performance. Quality evaluations are not made solely on the outcome results but on an involved evaluation of the process of service delivery.

The whole operating system of Total Quality Management is directed towards satisfying customer demand, and any obstacle in the way of achieving customer satisfaction must be removed. TQM places a greater emphasis on people within an organization and their role, through the spreading of their viewpoints and skills, through stimulating creativity, training and qualification, through the monitoring of tasks and seeking of ways to improve the quality of extended services. The emphasis is on teamwork and on the participation and motivation of employees, which requires certain changes in an organization's culture. What characterizes a TQM system is the understanding that quality is not only a technical function, but a systematic process as well, in which the whole organization is included. Quality must concern everyone and must be correctly established within the organization in order for such conditions to be created. All employees, and not only specialists, must participate in the improvement of quality. The organization must construct a quality management system which is clearly oriented towards the customer.

The service quality program involves a cooperative effort between marketing and operations. To develop quality service, a firm must follow certain principles. These ten principles of quality service offer a framework for a quality service program (Kotler et al., 1996: 364):

a. Leadership. The CEO of the organization must have a clear vision for the company, but it is not enough just to have a vision. The CEO must also communicate that vision and convince employees to believe in it and follow it;
b. Integrated Marketing throughout the Organization. The marketing concept states that marketing should be integrated throughout the organization;
c. Understand the Customer. Companies with quality products know what the market wants;
d. Understand the Business. Delivering quality services takes teamwork. Employees must realize how their jobs affect the rest of the team;
e. Apply Operational Fundamentals. The organization has to be well planned and managed;
f. Leverage the Freedom Factor. Employees must have the freedom to shape the delivery of the service to fit the needs of their guests;

g. Use Appropriate Technology. Technology should be used to monitor the environment, help operational systems, develop customer databases, and provide methods for communication with customers;
h. Good Human Resource Management. Employees must be capable of delivering the services promised to the customer;
i. Set Standards, Measure Performance and Establish Incentives. The most important way to improve service quality is to set service standards and goals and then teach them to employees and management;
j. Feedback the Results to the Employees. Employees should know what guests like and what they do not like. They should also know the areas that are improving and those that are not improving.

No unique method exists as to how to develop quality within a company. The way to total quality is different for each company, depending upon origin and the desired objectives. However, all companies undergo a similar journey and give importance to the same activities in order to develop a quality that satisfies their targeted market, which is confirmed by case studies. Specifically, a research of case studies revealed the following (Lockwood et al., 1996:156):

- that integrating quality into an organization and keeping it there, is no different and not separate, from the management of the organization as a whole. Well-managed firms tend to be good at managing quality
- quality is viewed by these companies as an integral part of the products offered
- in the successful firm, quality is integrated into the product offer, and the approach to quality is closely linked to a realistic perception of what the market wants
- control is also an important management function, no less important in the delivering of quality than in other aspects of management activity
- the subject of control raises questions about management style, corporate culture and motivation
- corporate change demands team-leadership skills, attention to motivation and usually a change in corporate culture
- every one of the case studies demonstrates the importance placed on training by organizations committed to service quality
- most of the case study companies found that an investment in people complements their strategies. In service industries particularly, the employees' performance can make a critical contribution to the customer's experience of the product.

The journey towards total quality will be different for each company. A company must decide which approach is best suited to the particular needs and culture of the organization and must find a way to implement it effectively.

The links between benchmarking and TQM are clear–establishing objectives based on industry best practice should directly contribute to the better meeting of internal and external requirements. Benchmarking shows the necessity of discontinuing current business methods and an orientation towards new and modified procedures. Simultaneously, it shows the various business levels of other companies, thereby directing the company towards more aggressive goals (Oakland, 1996: 181).

Technologies and conditions vary between different industries and markets, but the basic concepts of measurement and benchmarking are of general validity. The objective should be to produce products and services that conform to the requirements of the customer, geared towards never-ending improvements. The way to accomplish this is to use a continuous improvement cycle in all operating departments–nobody should be exempt. Measurement and benchmarking are not separate science or unique theories of quality management, but rather strategic approaches geared to getting the best out of people, processes, products, plant and programmes (Renko, et al., 1999: 11).

Globally, the influence of product quality on business rentability is being researched and analyzed. According to the data from a PIMS study (Profit Impact of Market Strategy) that processed information from over 2000 business entities on the influence of quality on the size of return for: (a) return on investment, ROI, (b) return on sales, ROS, there is a notably positive relationship between quality and business success. In this respect, ROI ranges from 12 to 32%, and ROS from 5 to 13% (Skoko, 2000: 38).

HOTEL EXCELSIOR

Hotel Excelsior was built in 1965. It is located near the Old Town of Dubrovnik, directly on a sea cliff facing the open sea and city walls. In 1997, the hotel was renovated and brought to a first category level, thereby becoming the first five-star hotel in Croatia. The speciality of Hotel Excelsior lies in the excellence of its services. After opening on September 04, 1998, the hotel was frequented by numerous local and foreign guests, and many delegations. The hotel held many congresses, meetings and symposiums, which justifies this investment and the appropriateness of a business policy geared towards the realization of results on the basis of highly-set criteria. The hotel placed considerable emphasis on keeping the quality it delivers in line with the growing expectations of its customers and the response of its competitors. Customer expectations have risen not just in the requirements for additional facilities, but in a more professional and flexible approach to customer needs, along with an emphasis on value for money.

The company's objective is to achieve and maintain competitive success in the five-star hotel sector. Its strategy is to deliver a consistent standard of service and product. The company's policy and initiatives on quality are in support of this. Keeping this in mind, as well as the experience obtained from using the ISO standards for five-star hotels, the hotel's management decided to introduce a system of quality according to HRN ISO 9002 norms in order to improve such criteria.

Benefits from registration to ISO 9000 can include (Downs, 1995: 21):

1. Tighter control over all aspects of the operation (particularly relevant considering the often chaotic nature of the industry)
2. Repeatability and consistency of product/service/hospitality
3. Staff are aware of their responsibilities and tasks and are trained to carry out their functions (particularly relevant in an industry where such reliance is placed on people)
4. Greater control over suppliers
5. Less waste
6. Inspection and test mechanisms to ensure due diligence

STANDARDS AND PROCEDURES

In Hotel Excelsior, quality is ensured by: the constant training of employees, the use of only selected procedures and work instructions, and the monitoring and control of the system. A quality manual was published in June 1999. The management of Hotel Excelsior assigned the necessary means and personnel required for setting up and maintaining a quality system. They also defined the need for training, equipment, and documented deviations in order to maintain the system's efficiency.

The director chose the person that will, alongside other duties, have authority to:

- ensure that the system of quality is established and maintained
- elaborate monthly reports on the state of the quality system
- report to the director on the quality system's performance so that the report could be used towards evaluating and improving the system
- maintain contact with a certification firm.

The responsibility matrix gives norms for the responsibility and authority of certain demands (see Figure 1).

The company director is responsible for ensuring that the efficiency of the quality system is re-examined. A management representative, assigned to

FIGURE 1. Responsibility Matrix

Function / Activities	1	2	3	4	5	6	7	8	9
Quality policy	P	S							
Supervision of the quality system	S	P							
Contract evaluation	P		S						
Contract evaluation (reservations)			P						
Management of documents and data		P							
Procurement									
Procurement of services	P	S		S	P	S			S
Process control-RECEPTION									
Process control-HOUSEHOLD							P		
Process control-KITCHEN						P			
Process control-SERVICES				P					
Process control-MAINTENANCE								P	
Control and testing		P							P
Discrepancies product	S	P	S						
Corrective and preventive action	S	P	S	S	S	S	S	S	S
Food storage			S	S	S	S	S	S	S
Beverage storage				P					
Household storage					P				
Management of quality reports		P				P			
Internal audits		P							
Training		P							
Statistical techniques		P							

Note:
1 – Director; 2 – QAM; 3 – Sales; 4 – Kitchen; 5 – Procurement; 6 – Household; 7 – Reception; 8 – Services; 9 - Maintenance
P – primary responsibility; S – secondary responsibility

quality, is responsible for the expert handling of an internal audit and the coordination of all functions dealing with the preparation, execution and functioning of the system. This person is also responsible for ensuring that corrective activities are introduced and for reporting to the management. Test reports made on the quality system are filed with the management representative responsible for quality.

Coordination for the preparation of reports is done by the management representative responsible for quality. Based upon an analysis of all elements, the management makes an assessment of on how efficient the quality system is in the realization of policies and set objectives, and on the corrective measures that should be undertaken to ensure improvements in the system.

The quality of a service is obtained through a controlled process that is developed prior to actually extending the service. Three main elements are needed for the quality of a service: a defined and documented process, trained employees and regular maintenance of equipment.

The management of documents and data is applied to all hotel documents:

- quality regulations
- procedures
- work instructions
- forms and other documents (external standards and so on).

A quality manual is prepared and compiled by the management representative responsible for quality, approved by the director. The procedures for the quality system are prepared and developed by department managers, verified by the management representative for quality, and approved by the director. Work instructions are prepared and developed by authorized department heads. They are reviewed by their co-workers, and are approved by the management representative for quality. The other documents of the quality system are prepared in separate areas of the organization, and they are reviewed and approved by the management representative on quality.

All those employed strive continuously towards self-improvement aimed towards the extension of excellent services and to the fulfillment of demands in the quality system. Hotel Excelsior educates its employees using the following kinds of seminars: foreign languages, internal auditors, computer training, professional seminars, internal and external courses. All employees have to be aware of those elements in the quality system that affect their work prior to the start of independent work.

Periodic equipment control is a basic part of planned maintenance. The technical maintenance service that is responsible for carrying out this procedure works out an appointment schedule for prevention control with accompanying instructions. Unplanned for standstills are avoided by the monitoring of equipment. This method effectively plans for spare parts, and the operations needed are carried out at the best possible moment. This procedure encompasses all machines, appliances, installations, and other equipment used for the normal running of a hotel.

Hotel Excelsior carries out an examination that is a basic part of the service process. It includes:

- evaluating and checking basic operations in order to avoid undesired tendencies and dissatisfied guests

- self-examination by staff giving the service as a basic part of the evaluation process
- a final evaluation by the guest in order to obtain the guest's view of the extended service.

Internal audit results are the basis for a re-examination of the quality system. An internal audit of the quality system is organized periodically in order to ensure an unbiased view of the quality system's efficiency. A QA manager is responsible for carrying out internal audits. This activity includes: (a) internal audit objectives; (b) internal audit planning; (c) internal audit frequency; (d) organizational units undergoing internal audit; (e) the field in which an internal audit is conducted; (f) reparation activities; (g) a report on the completed audit.

A QA manager prepares a list of areas that have to be documented. A QA manager carries out an audit or chooses and authorizes a specific person/persons. The person chosen is unaffiliated with the area under audit, and can be an external consultant. The auditor follows a written procedure on how the internal audit should be conducted that is prepared by the QA manager. The QA manager has to extend complete information in order for a successful audit. The auditor prepares a report that is given to the QA manager. The QA manager verifies all the reports and files a report that is a basic part of the management's evaluation.

The managers of departments showing inconsistencies are responsible for defining corrective measures, including deadlines and assigning responsibility for their completion. The hotel's management is responsible and is authorized for reviewing the quality of the system.

A guest's evaluation also measures the quality of services. A guest's reaction can be either immediate or postponed for later. For the evaluation of a guest's satisfaction, a measure has to be determined for service conditions that satisfy a guest's requirements, in order to reveal any possible discrepancies on how a hotel employee and guest view quality services. For this purpose, the hotel conducts surveys on the whole quality system by using specially prepared questionnaires.

Each month, the QA manager collects, analyzses and writes conclusive reports based upon the completed questionnaires. They have to be analyzed in case there are any claims and/or complaints and discrepancies concerning the extension of services or quality system, upon which appropriate measures have to be taken to rectify the situation. Preventive measures (for the prevention of such discrepancies in the future) and reparation activities are applied for the removal of discrepancies (these procedures are applied throughout the entire hotel). When discrepancies appear, the department manager that determined the discrepancy writes out a report that is then submitted to the QAM. After an analysis, they both determine the activities and the time period required to remedy the situation.

In case of an internal audit, the leader of an audit team completes a report on any discrepancies and defines what action/deadline is needed with the responsible person of the audited area. When the deadline for the completion of such action expires, the QAM checks out the efficiency of the action taken, and if satisfactory, closes the case. The QAM analyzes the discrepancy report and, if necessary, determines the preventive measures to be taken in order to avoid a repeat incident.

Internal audits are planned so that each segment of the system is audited at least once a year. Internal audits can also be conducted based on a decision made by the employer following an examination of the quality system or on the basis of complaints coming from guests/agencies (see Figure 2).

The management of Hotel Excelsior meets every three months in order to estimate the quality system. The trimester evaluation of the hotel's quality system is based upon:

- monthly reports submitted by the QA manager
- discrepancy reports filed during internal audits
- analyses of questionnaires on guest satisfaction
- guest complaints
- audit reports from certified establishments (bi-annually)
- analyses of seminars and training carried out (if any)
- analyses of changes resulting from new market strategies and social conditions.

A report is made during this meeting that is signed by the director and acting director of the hotel. The report contains observations, conclusions and recommendations as an outcome of the evaluations, and is used so that the management can undertake the action required for establishing a programme on service quality improvement.

MANAGEMENT AND CORPORATE CHANGE

At Excelsior, the gaining of an ISO 9002 registration for a renovated hotel was seen as the avoidance of adopting a five-star mentality from the start. Quality is seen as the key element in Excelsior's competitive strategy for the long-term development of their customer base. The benefits of ISO 9002 lie in its being a potential vehicle for the installing of disciplines of measurement,

FIGURE 2. An Internal Independent Estimate of Quality

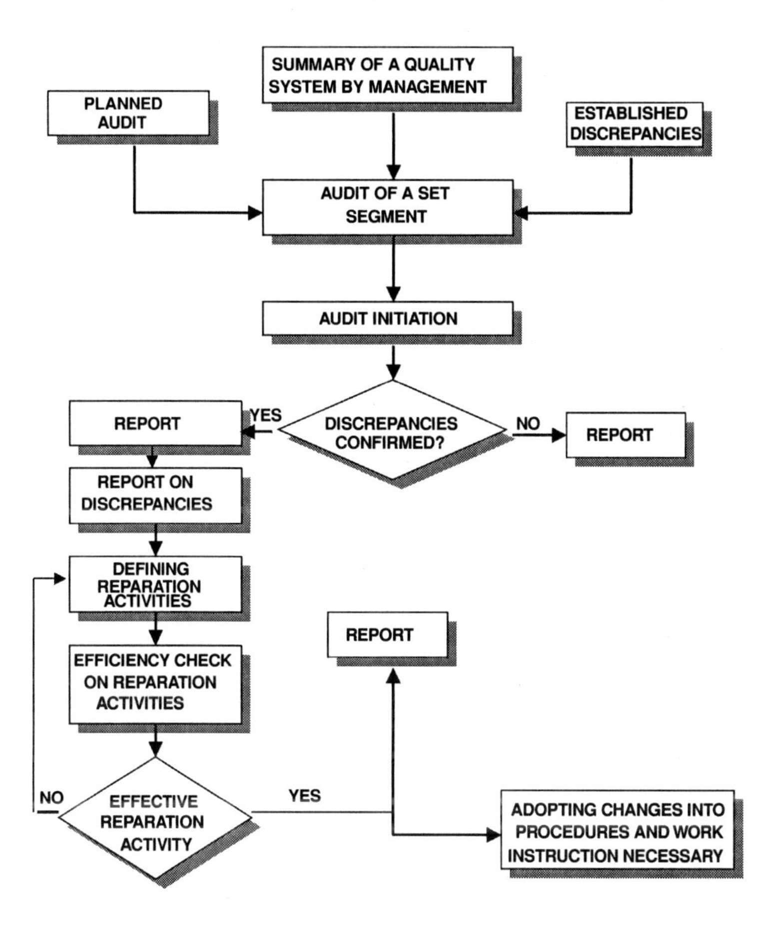

monitoring and control in place, and for the achieving of consistency of performance. The standard sets out how to establish, document and maintain an effective quality system that will prove to customers that the company is committed to quality and has the necessary systems and procedures in place to achieve it.

Hotel Excelsior has achieved a quality product through the consistently high performance of its staff. ISO registration ensured the gaining of several corporate objectives: good working conditions and effective communication at all levels, better understanding within the company, training programmes that help staff to develop their own skills, improvements in the quality of operations, etc.

Hotel Excelsior has recognized that the problems that can arise in service or production are typically not the result of one specific department or discipline. They are the result of a weak link in a service-delivery process that usually crosses over several different departments. As such, finding solutions to that weak link must require the input of a representative from each department involved. This, in turn, overcomes the traditional management hierarchy problem of the middle managers being unaware of a problem, and the front-line employees being incapable of fixing even the smallest problem to satisfy a customer immediately without management approval.

The success of Hotel Excelsior's commitment to teamwork has been brought about by their service strategy of linking employee empowerment and continuous improvement in customer service. Constantly examining and questioning the way things are done, helps everyone to be aware of the importance of delivering a quality service to the customer. Excelsior can show its trust and confidence in the abilities and experience of their employees by enabling employees to contribute ideas for improvement and to feel confident in solving a guest complaint immediately, rather than seeking the permission of a manager.

In Hotel Excelsior, interpersonal relationships are at a high and professional level. Everyone does their own work, the distribution of work tasks is quite clear, and everyone knows what is expected of them. New employees are given thorough instructions in order that they achieve the highest results possible and so that their personal interests can be identified with those of the company. Hotel employees are kept informed on the rate of business and are rewarded according to completed work.

In the hotel, great attention is paid to the way a guest is handled. Employees strive to foresee, recognize and satisfy a guest's needs. More often than not, they place themselves in the position of the guest in order to fulfill their tasks as much as possible. They treat their guests with the cordiality they themselves receive from their superiors.

The greatest benefit from the programme is the high level of consistency. The use of a teamwork approach from the outset has encouraged cooperation and discipline. Second, the senior staff in each department became more aware of the considerable work and commitment that would be involved–a documental procedure had to be written for every element of the duties and tasks their staff performed. Once everyone realized where they were going and how they were going to get there, everything began to fall into place.

Hotel Excelsior views its investment in people as a commitment towards achieving a quality product through the consistently high performance of its staff. Two specific corporate objectives are achieved: (a) good working conditions, effective communication at all levels, better understanding within the company, training programmes, thereby helping staff to develop their own skills, (b) support managers and other staff in using personal incentives to improve the quality of operation, recognition of the importance of genuine respect for all the individuals who comprise each employee team.

In 1999, the year the ISO standard was introduced, computer training courses were held for the administrative staff and sales department (12 personnel), internal auditor courses (10 personnel), foreign language courses (English and German Level II for 90 personnel and French and Italian Level I for 90 personnel), and a tour of other hotels was organized for professional staff members as a learning and exchange experience. During 2000, hotel employees were once again offered the opportunity of foreign language courses, professional educational courses, acquaintance with innovations in the hotel industry, and internal auditor courses.

The presence of formal systems and controls has a number of effects. For example, department heads realize that if they want to change a standard within their operation, then the change needs to be documented and approved. Quality meetings attended by department heads provide an opportunity to identify ways of improving performance and the steps needed to maintain quality standards.

Professional controls in Hotel Excelsior are carried out according to standards set out in the hotel and catering industry. For example, professional comments and recommendations related to kitchen work are given, that include an analysis and an opinion on food quality and the application of norms. Things that have been overlooked are pointed out and specific recommendations are made for their removal, which is important for the quality of overall hotel services. The kitchen manager has to discuss and correct discrepancies with personnel, and to emphasize successes as a good example. Controls are carried out daily, due to the nature of the work. For example, no food can leave the kitchen, and no room can be assigned to a guest prior to a completed control. Individual labor is ranked according to the quality of the service extended. Guest satisfaction and service quality are ranked on the basis of surveys.

An analysis of the surveys gathered indicates that the number of guest complaints has decreased following the introduction of the ISO standard. The most frequent complaints (almost half of the guests) were related to food quality, room tidiness and room service. The remaining guests were satisfied with the services offered. Today, the survey shows a very high level of guest satisfaction with the hotel. A managements report dated March 09, 2001 as to the functioning of the quality system notes that there are no customer complaints.

Further, ISO registration for Hotel Excelsior is an important market move to hold and expand the market share. It is difficult to judge in what measure this has affected sales and the use of capacity, as numerous other factors affect sales. However, it should not be forgotten that most tourists treat standard as a synonym for quality, which affects sales in any case. Table 1 shows some indicators on traffic trends for 1999 and 2000 (Statements of Assets and Liabilities, 2001).

Also, almost all departments have seen the advantages of ISO registration. In 2000, the realized turnover per sales outlet for the restaurant was 73.26%, for the tavern 17.06%, for the piano bar 44.53%, for the beach 37.96% and for the mini bar 44.53% up, as compared to the year 1999. The departments used ISO 9002 registration as a positive sales and marketing aid. The majority of guests recognized the standard as an indicator of quality. Further, in 2000, the hotel had the best food and beverage gross income as compared to the previous year (food gross income was 1.2 million USD and beverage gross income was 525 thousand USD).

With ISO 9002 the operation is successful in delivering a range of products and services that customers want in an efficient and effective way. But, there will always be ways of doing things a little bit better and effort should be spent looking for such continuous improvements. Even with these improvements, customer tastes are constantly changing and an operation must keep up to date with what the competitors are doing. In other words, the cycle needs to start again with customer research.

TABLE 1. Summary of Tourist Days in Hotel Excelsior

		1999	2000
TOURIST DAYS	Domestic	17 532	16 578
	Foreign	32 261	44 780
	Total	49 793	61 358
OCCUPANCY	Domestic	27.47%	15.05%
	Foreign	29.28%	40.65%
	Total	45.20%	55.70%
TOURIST DAYS PERCENTAGE	Domestic	35.21%	27.02%
	Foreign	64.79%	72.98%
NUMBER OF VISITORS	Domestic	5 969	5 673
	Foreign	11 059	13 460
	Total	17 028	19 133
AVERAGE ACCOMMODATION PER GUEST	Domestic	2.94	2.92
	Foreign	2.92	3.33
	Total	2.92	3.21

There is some evidence of ISO 9002's contribution to cost effectiveness. For example, the controls on suppliers provide assurance and performance records that can serve as a basis for decisions on reordering, choice of suppliers, including other service aspects, which in turn can affect costs, such as on-time deliveries. On the other hand, suppliers put in more effort for the hotel than for their other customers, as they are aware of the high controls and record-keeping of Hotel Excelsior. Stock control may also benefit from ISO 9002, as the less there is in stock, the less there is for the food and beverage manager to count. Also, this system enables the hotel to reduce wastage due to tighter controls and this does affect costs.

CONCLUSION

HRN EN 9002 does not guarantee improvements of quality, but the management of Hotel Excelsior believes that the systems and controls have this effect. Auditing, both external and internal, provides the opportunity to inspect each department and to ensure its efficient running. Both internal or external auditors will fail departments if they are not performing.

Through its commitment to ISO 9002, the company feels that they have made a strong statement about the importance of their people in providing a quality guest experience. The training programme has raised the quality and the managers feel that they are well on the way to developing a true culture within the organization.

Hotel Excelsior uses the ISO 9002 registration as a positive sales aid versus other hotels. Acquiring an ISO registration is an important market move, which enables a hold on the existing market share and which steers business away from hotels without registration. Consequently, the hotel gained considerable coverage in the trade press, although it is difficult to identify any tangible benefits. On the other hand, ISO 9002 contributed towards team building– everyone now knows what everyone should be doing and the process of achieving the objective has had its effect.

REFERENCES

Downs, V. (May 1995), Correspondence with the authors. West Region, BSI Quality Assurance.

Knowles, T. (1994), *Hospitality Management, An Introduction*. London: Pitman Publishing.

Kotler, P., Bowen, J., Makens, J. (1996), *Marketing for Hospitality & Tourism*. London: Prentice Hall International.

Lockwood, A., Baker, M., Ghillyer, A. (1996), *Quality Management in Hospitality*. London: Cassell.
Qakland, J.S. (1996), *Total Quality Management*. Oxford: Butterworth–Heineman.
Renko, N., Delić, S., Škrtić, M. (1999), Benchmarking u strategiji marketinga. Zagreb: MATE.
Skoko, H. (2000), Upravljanje kvalitetom. Zagreb: Sinergija d.o.o.
Statements of Assets and Liabilities, (January 2001), Dubrovnik: Hotel Excelsior d.d.

Serviced Accommodation, Environmental Performance and Benchmarks

David Leslie

SUMMARY. The establishment of benchmarks as a tool to aid the evaluation and review of the performance of hospitality and tourism enterprises in a number of areas, e.g., financial appraisal, grading schemes, is comparatively long established. More recently, benchmarks have been developed for the accreditation of business in such areas as TQM and IiP. One area that has been comparatively ignored is that of environmental performance of the enterprises. This is particularly notable, given the rise of attention and debate over sustainable development and the need for a balance between economic growth and the quality of the environment which has generated much debate.

The quintessential importance of this latter aspect–the quality of the environment–to the development of tourism has long been recognised, and since the mid-1980s has generated substantial attention to the impact of tourism on the physical environment. In combination, this attention has led to the development of 'sustainability indicators for tourist destinations.' However, there has been a substantial lack of attention to the environmental performance of the enterprises involved and their impacts on the environment–taken in its widest senses.

David Leslie is Reader in Tourism, Tourism, Travel and Hospitality, Division of Management, Caledonian Business School, Glasgow Caledonian University, Cowcaddens Road, Glasgow G4 OBA (E-mail: D.Leslie@gcal.ac.uk).

[Haworth co-indexing entry note]: "Serviced Accommodation, Environmental Performance and Benchmarks." Leslie, David. Co-published simultaneously in *Journal of Quality Assurance in Hospitality & Tourism* (The Haworth Hospitality Press, an imprint of The Haworth Press, Inc.) Vol. 2, No. 3/4, 2001, pp. 127-147; and: *Benchmarks in Hospitality and Tourism* (ed: Sungsoo Pyo) The Haworth Hospitality Press, an imprint of The Haworth Press, Inc., 2001, pp. 127-147. Single or multiple copies of this article are available for a fee from The Haworth Document Delivery Service [1-800-HAWORTH, 9:00 a.m. - 5:00 p.m. (EST). E-mail address: getinfo@haworthpressinc.com].

This weakness, and the absence of suitable benchmarks, emerged in the initial stages of a major project designed to evaluate the environmental performance of the tourism sector in the Lake District of England; an area listed in the top 50 of the most attractive tourist destinations in the world in 2000. Thus, the first stage of the project required the development of a set of suitable indicators designed to assess the environmental performance of the enterprises involved. This article discusses the development and derivation of these indicators, with specific focus on serviced accommodation, and subsequently the establishment of a range of benchmarks which may not only be applied in evaluating progress in future assessment of the environmental performance of this sector in the Lake District but also may be applied in other destinations throughout the world.

KEYWORDS. Serviced accommodation, tourism enterprises, benchmarks environmental performance, environmental management, indicators, going green

INTRODUCTION

Benchmarks are undoubtedly valuable in assessing the performance of the operations in one area or another of any hospitality or tourism business, and particularly so for comparative purposes. In the case of tourism destinations, steps have already been taken to establish 'sustainability indicators' which are designed to provide insights into how the destination is developing in terms of sustainable development. However, what is missing is attention to the environmental performance of the supply side, as represented by tourism enterprises within tourist destinations. Thus, whilst it is possible potentially to assess the combined performance of tourism enterprises by using the collective results of benchmarking in a number of areas, it is not possible to establish the overall performance of the same enterprises using environmental performance benchmarks. In the first instance, there is thus a need for a range of indicators to be established and applied to tourism enterprises which can then be used to formulate appropriate environmental performance benchmarks, not only for assessing individual operations but also in terms of a destination locality.

A number of projects on indicators for tourism have been initiated [see Leslie, 1998]. In 1996, indicators for 'sustainable tourism' were developed [WTO, 1996]. The English Tourism Council is also currently working on the development of indicators for tourism destinations. To date, these appear to pay very limited attention to tourism enterprises and their operational environment. As yet there are no widely accepted indicators for tourism enterprises. Therefore, it is highly appropriate that such indicators were devised for a study of tourism enterprises in the Lake District National Park.

The significance of this study primarily serves to establish the current situation regarding the collective environmental performance of tourism enterprises, and incorporated wider dimensions of sustainable development, through the development and application of indicators to assess the environmental performance of those enterprises. The findings, most significantly in this context, thus serve to establish a foundation range of benchmarks on which to base assessment in the future of progress in this area and contribute to the development of policy and actions to influence such progress in any tourist destination.

The project, on which this article is based, is far too extensive to convey given the constraints of space. Thus, the aim here is to establish briefly the rationale underpinning the need for and the approach adopted to establish environmental performance benchmarks. The project is then introduced with specific reference to serviced accommodation operations and subsequently the case area. The indicators established and a range of findings are then presented, followed by a number of the emergent implications prior to the concluding points.

THE NEED FOR ENVIRONMENTAL PERFORMANCE BENCHMARKS

In the latter years of the twentieth century concerns over the quality of the environment gained significant attention from local to global levels. In the 1990s as environmental concerns increased, pressure mounted . . . 'on industry to address the actual and potential contribution of their operations in contributing to environmental degradation and develop systems to assess the environmental performance of individual operations-enterprises [Welford & Starkey, 1996:xi].' Further reinforcement of this came from the UK Roundtable on Sustainable Development: 'A number of the pressing problems identified [earlier] including climate change, traffic patterns and waste, will require significant behavioral change by businesses and the general public as well as by government. There is still widespread ignorance about the nature of some of these problems and the need for more sustainable solutions' [DETR, 2000:10 para.41]. The tourism sector is no less susceptible than is any other sector of the economy to these changes. Furthermore, . . . 'the industry and tourists individually are being expected and required to shoulder more responsibility for the effects of travel and behaviour on host communities, both physical and human' [Butler, 1993:5]. To further such aims, government departments should 'establish systems and procedures to incorporate sustainable development considerations at the core of the decision making process and to identify actions necessary to bring sustainable tourism development into being [WTTC et al., 1996]. Furthermore 'private interests, as they benefit from visitor spending, should invest in protecting and enhancing the local environment,' a factor not only identified by the Countryside Commission [now Countryside Agency] but considered to be one of the critical areas 'on which a sustainable countryside will ultimately hinge' [CC, 1993:6].

In response to these challenges, there is a need for tourism enterprises not to be treated solely in terms of their products/services, but in the wider context of their external environment. These enterprises draw on local resources and through the production and delivery of services return pollution and waste back into the locality. Thus, pressure rises on the locality to handle these by-products. If tourism and the locality is to be sustained, 'It is thus essential to reduce the consumption of resources and to establish means by which the industry's wastes and resulting environmental impacts can be reduced, thereby approaching a state where a balance can be achieved between environmental exploitation and consumer utility' [Wallis & Woodward, 1997:95]. It is therefore essential for all enterprises and those organisations involved in tourism–as well as the visitors themselves–to address these issues of resource usage, consumption and waste; a view recognised recently in the need to: 'promote better understanding among operators of the business benefits available from programmes to reduce energy consumption, waste production and water use' [DCMS, 1999:59]. The environmental performance–the environmental management and operational practices–of tourism enterprises, therefore, is very much a part of today's agenda. In effect, this means the adoption of what are perceived as environmentally friendly management and operational practices. In other words, the 'greening' of the tourism sector, which is essentially no more than the positioning of the sector to respond to the emerging environmental challenge which will be a key issue of the 21st Century.

Addressing the environmental performance of tourism enterprises has and is being promoted by an increasing range of organisations. These organisations range from international players in the tourism sector to a host of public sector and non-governmental organisations. Significantly, a number of such organisations have been promoting aspects of environmental management since the early 1990s; for example, Department of Environment and English Tourist Board [DoE & ETB, 1991:5], and the Rural Development Commission et al. in 1991 [RDC, ETB & CC, 1991], the Countryside Commission in 1993 [CC, 1993:6] and the Hotel and Catering International Management Association [HCIMA], though, as noted below, with little success. Partly accounting for this is: '. . . that tourism is viewed primarily as a private sector activity. The adoption of environmentally responsible action in respect of current business operations is still largely perceived as a matter for individual firms' [Goodall, 1994:30]. Further 'Many managers are pretty confident that environmental issues don't affect their business' [CEBIS,1996]. As such, they are the least likely to go out of their way to get information, yet are possibly the managers who most need environmental advice.

TOURISM ENTERPRISES AND ENVIRONMENTAL PERFORMANCE

The most frequently cited process of assessing the environmental performance of an enterprise is environmental auditing, defined as 'a management tool comprising a systematic, documented, periodic and objective evaluation of the performance of the organisation, management system and processes designed to protect the environment' [Goodall, 1994:30]. Environmental Auditing is a form of self-regulation because it is not mandatory to adopt such an approach to becoming more environmentally responsible.

A key factor in adopting environmental auditing is the recognition by the owners of businesses that they should address the environmental performance of their own businesses. Of a number of environmental management techniques which can be adopted, the three major ones are: BS 7750; Eco-Management and Audit Scheme [EMAS]; and ISO 14001. However, these methods are not necessarily appropriate to small enterprises, particularly 'micro-businesses' due to their scope and potential costs. The aim here is therefore to identify those environmental management initiatives designed to promote and encourage the adoption of environmental management and adoption of 'environmentally friendly' practices; in other words the 'greening' of tourism enterprises. The most reknown initiatives are: The International Hotels Environment Initiative (IHEI) [see Black, 1995], Green Globe [see Hawkins, 1995], the Green Audit Kit [see RDC, 1996], and, in Scotland, the Green Business Scheme. Other more localised schemes include Little Acorns LA21 Tourism Kit [NFDC, 1998] and The Green Lantern [LCC, 1999].

However, though the potential of these initiatives in promoting the adoption of appropriate actions is recognised, it is substantially restricted to the major players in the marketplace and as such fails to reach the plethora of small independent enterprises which collectively constitute the major proportion of tourism supply.

MEASURING PROGRESS: ENVIRONMENTAL INDICATORS FOR TOURISM ENTERPRISES

Over the last decade, leading national organisations have been involved directly or indirectly, through their policies, in seeking to promote initiatives designed to address aspects of environmental performance, e.g., energy consumption, waste reduction and local purchasing. Therefore, to establish the environmental performance of the tourism enterprises, at first glance, it may appear sufficient to investigate their level of awareness and responses to the range of measures collectively promoted in those policy documents and by professional associations directly involved in tourism. Though providing valuable insights into how well these policies have been implemented, it would have been of limited value in terms of establishing the current situation, the challenges and the opportunities. Therefore, a more comprehensive approach needs to be formulated, an approach which provides in effect, a 'state of the art' review of the environmental performance of tourism enterprises in a popular tourist destination in order to establish the current position regarding progress towards greater sustainability.

The key question is how is the environmental performance of these enterprises to be measured, and in particular, 'If we cannot measure it, how will we know when or if we have made progress?'[Brandon, 2000]. In effect, this means addressing what is increasingly recognised as the 'triple bottom line'– that the economic, environmental and social benefits are achieved in equal measure. There has been much discussion on this and the need to establish objective measures which will stand the test of time which has led to the emergence of 'sustainability indicators' which, for the most part, has been undertaken in the broad context of society and with limited attention to tourism.

The first step in developing such indicators is to establish what makes a good indicator. With the criteria established by the DoE [1996:11] in mind, the first stage to establish the environmental performance indicators involved a review of an extensive range of publications and initiatives relating to the 'greening' of tourism. To help guide the formulation and scope of these indicators, due consideration was given to the three dimensions of sustainable development–the local economy, environment and the community. In essence, therefore, an approach which included attention to ways through which tourist-generated revenues find their way back into the local economy, and which will inform the development of 'a wise growth strategy for tourism . . . which integrates the economic, social and environmental implications of tourism and which spreads the benefits throughout society as widely as possible' [DCMS, 1999:48]. The development of these indicators was also informed by those areas for action identified and prioritised by the WTTC et al. [1996]. Consideration was also given to the involvement of tourists and promotion of awareness of environmental practices and involvement in conservation schemes. Further, the main elements of environmental auditing, e.g., use of resources, waste management, were taken into account.

The indicators so derived were then applied in the undertaking of a substantive study to assess the environmental performance of the tourism sector in the Lake District National Park [LDNP]. These indicators have been categorised into sections and are presented below in the context of the findings.

THE CASE STUDY

The overall objective of the study was to assess the environmental performance, including sustainability, of the tourism sector in the Lake District National Park [Cumbria, England] and the extent to which policies advocating 'the greening of tourism' and related initiatives have been realised. Primarily, the focus was on the serviced accommodation sector in recognition of its significance in terms of the volume and value of tourism to a destination. In particular, the study aimed:

- to identify and evaluate the level of awareness, attitudes and perceptions of green issues, and associated practices, of those involved in the serviced accommodation sector
- to identify the management practices and operations of the serviced accommodation sector.

The methodology derived for the study involved the design of a postal survey and subsequent more detailed investigations [in effect environmental audits] designed to establish the approach and actual practices of those involved in the management of accommodation operations based on the derived indicators. Further, the survey sought to establish key influential factors which either help or hinder the adoption of such practices. A total of 230 (27%) completed questionnaires were received–see Table 1.

TABLE 1. Surveys and Returns: Serviced Accommodation

Category	Database	Responses	Responses (%)
Hotels	303	36	12
Inns	23	17	74
Guests Houses	266	93	34
B&B	261	84	32
Total	853	230	27

THE LAKE DISTRICT NATIONAL PARK AND TOURISM

The LDNP is a part of Cumbria, a rural area with a population of 440,000 people, and is less than half of the area. Approximately 10% of Cumbria's population lives in the LDNP, partly clustered around the Parishes of Windermere, Keswick and Ambleside–the major tourism 'honey pots' [LDNPA, 1997 & 1998]. These areas are easily accessible to the great majority of visitors who arrive and travel within the National Park by car [90%] [LDNPA, 1998]. Although figures vary, it is estimated that one third of employed residents are largely dependent upon the needs and activities of these visitors, an indicator of which is evidenced by the 65,000 [approximately] bed spaces [LDNPA, 1997].

The volume and value of tourism to the area is shown in Table 2, and visitor spending by sector is presented in Table 3. The significance of these figures is manifest in the estimated number of jobs supported by tourism in Cumbria, which has been cited as approximately 10% of the population at 42,000 [Collier, 2000], 50% of which are located in the LDNP, compared to about 6% nationally [Leslie, 2001]. In addition to direct employment, tourism supports local services, for example, the bus and rail network, village shops and public houses; and support for many retail outlets [Cole, 1999]. The importance of this contribution is well-illustrated by various comments made by participants in the study e.g., 'Most jobs come from tourism,' 'The community benefits from tourism' and 'The community and countryside relies on tourism.'

Table 3 illustrates the significant role that the accommodation and catering sector play in tourism supply as well as their significance in terms of influence on the volume and value of tourism supply in these sectors to a locality. [Manifest in their substantial proportional share (60% or more) of visitors spend]. Overall, of the 30,000 businesses considered to be involved in tourism supply, only one employs over 250 staff; 85% employ fewer than 10 staff [Collier, 2000]. It is particularly striking that the tourism supply in Cumbria is provided to a great extent by small enterprises known as micro-businesses which are particularly significant given that their 'actions impact daily upon sustainability issues' [Becker et al., 1999].

TABLE 2. Volume and Value of Tourism to Cumbria

Category	UK Residents	Overseas Residents
Trips (mn)	2.9	0.29
- holiday - VFR - business	77% 8% 11%	69% 19% 7%
Nights (mn)	11.5	1.4
Spending (£mn)	380	49
Accommodation - hotel, guesthouse	28	70
Day Visits - trips (mn) - spending (£mn)	9 107	

Source: ETC [1999] drawn from ETC, NITB, STB and WTB. [1999]

Notes to Table 2.
- the majority of UK residents [24%] are from North West England and Merseyside.
- revenues: short breaks account for 9%; holidays 38%
- 'no activity' is undertaken by 30%; 44% cite hiking/walking
- day visitors account for 73% of all trips and 20% of total visitor spending.

TABLE 3. Visitor Spending by Sector (%)

Sector	Day Visitors *	Domestic Tourists #
Accommodation	-	37
Retail	12	11
Catering	60	26
Attraction	13	5
Travel	16	20

Note: minor differences in summation reflect rounding errors
Source: Leslie, 2001

It is clear from the above that the LDNP has a substantial tourism economy, and therefore, as a destination, it is a very appropriate case for the establishment of benchmarks for assessing the environmental performance of tourism supply in a destination.

THE INDICATORS AND FINDINGS

In the light of space constraints and interests of brevity, it is not possible to explain all the indicators nor to provide all the results. Thus, the approach adopted identifies the main categories and associated indicators, with explanatory commentary on some of the indicators possibly less obvious ones, and presents a selection of the more significant results. These findings serve well to convey the scope of the indicators and the overall environmental performance of the serviced accommodation sector.

Profile of the Accommodation Operations

A generally recognised feature of tourism development is that in its primary stage the 'product' is essentially highly localised. However, as it develops, the general trend is that demand increases and supply expands leading to inward investment by external companies and increasing imports to the area to expand supply and meet visitor needs. Therefore, it is all the more important to investigate the extent to which tourism enterprises are locally owned and managed and the level of interconnections with other sectors of the economy and the community, as well as considering the operational aspects of enterprises in terms of environmental performance; in other words, the triple bottom line. This is also important because sustainable development is about achieving a balance between economic development and the environment and equity amongst the community. Thus the 'health' of the businesses involved is important.

The indicators: location; ownership; category; period in operation; location of owners; occupancy: changes in the level of business activity in the last five years; seasonality and variances over the last five years; guest rooms: range and type of facilities in room; plans for development.

- The majority of enterprises are owner, managed, and have fewer than ten rooms, the majority of which reflect today's guest expectations of suites with televisions and beverages facilities and, not surprisingly, are located in the 'honey-pot' areas.
- There was a particularly high response rate from relatively new market entrants, i.e., owners who have been operating for less than five years [1 in 4], which might suggest that newer market entrants have a greater interest in the environmental performance of their operation.
- Approximately half of the enterprises indicated an increase in demand over the last five years with slightly less indicating an increase in profitability. Reasons for such increases were found to be more attributed to improvements in delivery of services and promotion rather than increased demand. The overall indications that there has been no marked increase in visitor demand is reflected in the finding that there has been only a slight increase in employment over the last five years.

- Seasonality: approximately three-quarters of the enterprises are open throughout the year, which is reflected in the comparatively limited number of opportunities for seasonal employment.
- Many of the enterprises have current plans for developing their business in one way or another. These plans, coupled with regular repairs and maintenance [evident from the high standard of visual presentation of many enterprises], generate substantial work for local builders and tradespeople.

AWARENESS, PERCEPTIONS AND ATTITUDES OF OWNERS

The significance of promoting awareness of and involvement in LA21 is that it is targeted at all members of the community and serves to inform them about sustainable development and seeking the balance between the economy, the people and the environment. Therefore given that the majority of all the enterprises are managed by the owners-members of the community–then this is potentially a substantial conduit in encouraging attention to the environmental performance of the enterprise. Thus, the owners and managers of tourism enterprises should also have been encouraged indirectly to adopt the practices of sustainable development through developing an awareness and knowledge of LA21. The indicators also serve to establish to what extent the initiatives and related practices promoted in a range of policies for tourism and the countryside launched predominantly in the early 1990s have been realised.

Indicators: awareness of related initiatives; perceptions of potential factors of influence; attitudes to impacts of sector; support for local conservation groups; participation in conservation schemes/initiatives membership of conservation organisations and local community groups.

- In general there are low levels of awareness of environmental management systems and practices, policies and 'green' initiatives; as evidenced by the substantial lack of awareness of LA21 [nine out of ten participants]. There is little involvement, generally less than one in ten (except for the National Trust), in professional associations and 'green' organisations through which owners/managers may have developed awareness of such initiatives. Membership of tourism related organisations was also found to be very limited with the exception of the Cumbria Tourist Board [CTB]. Approximately one in ten enterprises did indicate awareness of the Green Audit Kit which has been promoted by the Cumbria Tourist Board yet one in seven were found to be members!

- Approximately one in six of the enterprises are involved in a 'green' scheme in one form or another though mainly the Tourism and Conservation Partnership. A finding which is perhaps surprising as such support has been advocated for much of the 1990s.
- Owners were found neither to agree nor disagree that the accommodation sector has an impact on the environment and if customers are interested in whether an enterprise is or is not 'green.'
- Environmental reporting was not considered important whereas addressing customer complaints, improving profitability and achieving budgets were all considered to be 'important/very important.'
- 'Customer care' and 'cost savings' were considered most important influences on the adoption of more environmentally-friendly practices. Factors considered the least important were 'industry standards' and 'competitors' actions.' The introduction of a Government policy to adopt such measures was considered the most likely influence to have an effect.

STAFFING

Indicators: fulltime, part time; area of residence; maintenance of quality and quantity of staff over the last five years; variances to number of employees over the last five years; recruitment: local people favoured; training and development: encourage staff development.

- The majority of the enterprises employ fewer than ten staff.
- Whilst employers generally favour recruiting local people they find difficulties in recruiting local staff due to lack of interest in non-skilled positions, difficulties of getting to the enterprise, and problems in finding suitable local accommodation. To overcome such difficulties many employers provide accommodation for staff as well as importing staff from outside the region. This is reflected in the findings that approximately two thirds of full-time staff and one third of part-time staff are drawn from outside of the LDNP.

ENVIRONMENTAL MANAGEMENT

Indicators: environmental policy and environmental auditing; monitoring of environmental performance; monitoring of energy consumption; monitoring of general waste; internal design elements introduced to reduce energy consumption/waste; insulation; eco-labelling of equipment, e.g., low energy; equipment energy labelled for efficiency; laundry/housekeeping practices; cleaning materials and washing agents; policy for energy management; sources of energy; energy and waste management practices; use of recycled products; waste separated for recycling.

- There is limited formalised [e.g., a written policy] attention to the environmental performance of many of the enterprises and comparatively few operations have a written environmental policy, although overall there appears to be a distinct awareness of general energy efficiency practices e.g., roof insulation, time-controlled central heating. The size and scale of the operation is often an influential factor in that the smaller the enterprise, the more likely formal procedures will be absent. However, the introduction of measures such as energy efficient lighting systems and measures to reduce water consumption is very limited. The absence of formal statements does not preclude attention to environmental performance, since one in four of enterprises indicated that they monitor some aspects of their operations, e.g., electricity and gas, and, though to a lesser extent, waste [rubbish].
- Few operators have introduced more energy-efficient systems for central heating, either through a lack of awareness of such systems or cost. The design of combined heat and power units for smaller operations are being developed and these should be available for adoption in the near future. The Government's introduction of an energy tax on consumption should encourage further developments in this area.
- The use of more energy-efficient equipment, e.g., eco-labelled fridges and dishwashers, is increasing as older equipment is replaced. The increasing availability of 'environmentally benign' washing powders and cleaning materials is evident from their use by the majority of audited enterprises.
- Recycling was identified as a major issue by many respondents; inadequate facilities, lack of information and poor access were cited as the main problems.

PURCHASING POLICIES, PATTERNS AND PRACTICES

The purchase of produce and products produced within the area is important as this supports other enterprises and sectors of the local economy. Further, such practice helps reduce the importation of goods into the area and thus leakages from the local economy. Further, such support of local suppliers/retailers helps to maintain, or increase, the range of provisions as well as contributing to their viability.

Indicators: purchasing policy; choice of supplies and suppliers, use of pre-packed portioned products, local products/produce favoured; environmental policy of suppliers requested

- An orientation to variable costs is most in evidence in purchasing behaviour. The purchasing patterns of enterprises are largely a function of individual size and scale, i.e., many shop for convenience as and when required. In general, purchasing tends to be from suppliers based within the LDNP and predominantly from 'local' outlets. As such, they reflect the general pattern of today's householders in that most supplies are bought from major outlets in the area, e.g., supermarkets versus local shops, generally available products versus more locally produced products.
- There is a limited level of awareness of what local produce and products are available within the area and a wider range of local produce and products available than is generally known. Fresh produce from local producers is the least likely purchase. The majority of enterprises indicated they favour and would prefer to purchase local produce and products which reflects the growing attention to the significance of using locally produced goods and services [see MAFF, 2000]. Factors cited, militating against locally produced produce and products are: cost, quality, consistency and availability.

GUESTS

Indicators: accessible by public transport; access; means of arrival by guests; is environmental awareness promoted; promotion of environmentally-friendly actions/activities; promotional material

- Owners/managers appear to be more reactive to perceived needs and interests of their guests rather than being proactive and encouraging them to be more aware and 'environmentally friendly' in their behaviour.
- Four out of every five enterprises claim to encourage their guests to arrive by public transport. However, the majority of guests [approx. 90%] arrive at the enterprise by car.
- Enterprises generally do not promote environmental awareness and action. Those operations which do tend to promote energy conservation, e.g., reuse towels rather than change them on a daily basis during a guest's stay.

- Whilst the enterprises predominantly provide a wide range of standard promotional material for visitors, there is an evident lack of information for guests on 'visitor payback schemes,' e.g., Tourism and Conservation Partnership.

The findings confirm that the tourism sector is a key player in the economy, the environment and the community of the LDNP. However, it is also evident that there is substantial scope for enhancing this role and developing the environmental performance of the sector. Quintessentially tourism enterprises are managed by people who predominantly live and work in the LDNP. It is people's behaviour, attitudes and values that lead to environmental performance appraisal, as well exemplified by the findings. Thus, these findings are not unexpected and bring into question the efficacy of national policies. They effectively demonstrate that the policies presented by the leading bodies involved are often little more than rhetoric on 'good practice.'

Progress towards a 'greener' tourism sector and a more sustainable community in the long term is not only being promoted now but will become more important as the century unfolds. In terms of sustainability, it is important that the local economy is as diverse as possible and in this tourism has a key role to play in developing much stronger linkages with other sectors and in promoting greater production and utilisation of local produce and products thereby contributing to a stronger economy with more opportunities for employment and thereby reducing dependency on tourism. Through such development the area will be far better positioned to withstand fluctuations in demand and a shift in fashion; as well as addressing any opportunities and threats that may arise.

IMPLICATIONS

On the basis of the foregoing findings, it is evident that to develop effective benchmarks for assessing the environmental performance of serviced accommodation and, more widely, tourism enterprises *per se,* in a destination there is a need to address those factors of significance which can and will influence both attention to, and the success of, any initiative designed to promote the introduction and adoption of such benchmarks. Thus, a number of the more significant outcomes of the study which have implications for the successful introduction of benchmarks for environmental performance are identified and discussed.

Ineffectiveness of Lead Agencies

The findings of this study bring into question the efficacy of those policies and initiatives, designed to improve the environmental performance of the tourism enterprises. Government, both central and local, have been largely ineffective given that the former has been advocating the 'greening of tourism' since the start of the 1990s, a position taken up by the network of National and Regional Tourist Boards, whilst local government has been charged with developing Local Agenda 21 plans since 1992. Such ineffectiveness is not limited to government and related agencies with involvement in tourism, but also the professional associations such as the HCIMA. An exemplar of this, if not *the* exemplar, is the lack of awareness of, and adoption of the principles and practices contained within, the Green Audit Kit despite its identification and promotion in a number of policy documents since the mid-1990s, including those of the CTB since the late nineties.

A Weakness of Environmental Management Initiatives

Responses suggest that, although many enterprises consider that they are committed to environmental management, this commitment is overshadowed by greater attention to attaining maximum financial returns through the adoption of good housekeeping policies. Findings from the attitudinal questions support this and evidence a degree of cynicism and a large amount of ambivalence to 'green' ideas, environmental impacts and related initiatives. However, although there are signs of progress there is a clear need for more direct encouragement and promotion. As the Countryside Agency argue, ways must be developed 'to encourage new and existing tourism businesses to adopt socially and environmentally sustainable practice' [CA, 2000; and ETC/CA, 2000].

Seasonality

The implications arising from the fact that the majority of the enterprises do not close during the quieter periods of November to March are that the gradual spread of season will help to sustain local businesses, and thereby retain staff, throughout the year. On the other hand, and although beneficial to the economy [in particular, suppliers to enterprises], expansion of the season may exacerbate disbenefits in other areas. Thus, it is all the more important that the enterprises involved address and seek to improve their environmental performance.

Community Involvement in Planning and Development

The objective of 'greener' tourism enterprises demands that they operate in more sustainable ways, developing and building on more extensive links with other sectors of the localities economy and with the local community more generally. However, given that individual environmental awareness and practice is limited indicates that there is clearly no collective commitment to cultural and social sustainability [see Cole, 1999]. This lack of *collective* commitment suggests that a "community approach" faces challenges, because the community approach must inherently be collective.

Local Produce and Local Products

The purchase of arts and crafts, whether for decoration, display or use in the provision of services, also contributes to the local economy. Purchasers appear to favour personal gain, e.g., cost savings, rather than spreading the benefit to the local community. The enterprises in general could, and in terms of sustainability should, be addressing their environmental performance in this area and increasing their demand for locally produced produce and products.

Recycling

A major area highlighted are obstacles which restrict the potential to increase the range, and quantity, of materials for recycling; difficulties identified included an apparent lack of facilities, access-from an enterprise to recycling points and insufficient provision of information on how to recycle products. By addressing these factors there would potentially be a greater commitment and involvement from those enterprises not currently involved in recycling activities. This is important to many visitors; for example, one family from Germany asked their 'host' where the facility was for recycling batteries. This area needs to be improved in order to facilitate recycling of materials such as plastic and cans–not only glass. The latest government initiatives such as the introduction of new statutory targets for recycling may well stimulate such actions [see Joy, 2000; and DETR, 2000].

Visitors–Accommodation Guests

The lack of responsiveness to the purported trend in 'green consumerism' is also evident from the responses to the attitudinal questions and further enquiries in the auditing stage. Few contributors were as sure as the respondent who, in response to the question on whether they seek to attract 'green' guests, said:

Yes, people are very sensitive here. One respondent indicated that he had sought the advice of the CTB regarding where best to advertise for green tourists and was disappointed by the absence of any advice. In marked contrast comments offered in response to the question as to what factors may discourage you from adopting more environmentally friendly practices: *90% of tour ists would not adjust their holiday arrangements for environmental issues* and *Guests are not interested.* However, guests could be encouraged, and themselves be encouraging of enterprises, to make greater use of local produce and products.

CONCLUSION

Progress by tourism enterprises in addressing the environmental performance is very slow, despite the fact that there has and continues to be an ever-growing range of initiatives, literature and advice, much of which is non-sectoral specific and thus of general application, promoting attention to this area throughout the 1990s and particularly in the last two years [for example, see Forte, 2000]. That more progress has not been made serves to reinforce the view that the availability of literature and/or advice is not itself sufficient to engender positive action.

However, as the findings attest, awareness is not THE key factor, but rather it is the attitudes and values of the individual–the enterprises' owners–which, combined with their knowledge and understanding of environmental issues and related practices, is the key influence in terms of taking appropriate actions. 'Nevertheless some progress can, and should be made certainly with respect to the relatively simple issues of paper use, water use, recycling and energy efficiency. A simple environmental auditing process can achieve worthwhile results with clear economic gains' [PTC (Jersey), 1998]. In other words, the introduction of environmental performance benchmarks.

More problematic is how to encourage the myriad of tourism enterprises to put environmental concerns, and the adoption of 'environmentally friendly' management practices, to the forefront of their business operations and strategic decisions. A factor which will certainly play a part in the wider adoption of such a process is the possibility of legislation which directly targets energy consumption and waste, and the influence of consumer pressure groups [see Osborn, 2000]. In the interim, it is particularly reassuring that progress is reflected in the genuine interest demonstrated by many owners of serviced accommodation enterprises and in subsequent discussions; especially in the audits. Evidently there are many persons who are developing attention to 'environmentally friendly practices' and the environmental performance of their enterprise. These persons and enterprises, along with potentially many other enterprises, will respond positively to effective promotion of environmental management systems and initiatives designed to promote and further develop linkages with the economy, environment and community. But this will only happen through increased awareness of the 'why,' 'what' and 'how' involved in addressing environmental performance and as long as such 'messages' are presented in the right way, i.e., positively with the right message.

Looking to the Future

The long-term sustainability of the community in the LDNP will depend on an economic base which is as diverse as possible. It is, therefore, very important that tourism continues to bolster the economy, but this should be one of many economic activities. Given the current strength of tourism's economic contribution there is a very real danger of over reliance on this sector and the loss of sight of the need to ensure a diversified economy. This is important in the event that tourism demand does not increase and all the more important if demand declines. Even if such a decline is short term; witness the impact of the fuel supply 'crisis' in mid-September [2000] and more significantly, the foot and mouth crisis in Spring 2001.

In total, the findings provide a valuable and independent audit of the current position of the environmental performance of tourism enterprises in a very popular destination. In effect, the data gained in response to the indicators will serve well as a baseline set of benchmarks against which to assess progress in the future.

The adoption of the benchmarks arising from the results of the performance indices developed for this study, the setting of targets for improvements and the establishment and implementation of appropriate actions to achieve those targets will go someway to help ameliorate the impact of such events. Indeed, the adoption of these benchmarks will inform the development of any popular tourist destination and in so doing help the area's ability to withstand a decline in demand and, more significantly, contribute to the sustainability of the area's economy and environment.

REFERENCES

Becker, H., Dunn, S. and Middleton V.T.C. [1999], *'Think Small–Think Local–Think Micro-Businesses: A First Report for Consultation and Endorsement*, August.

Black, C.W. [1995] The Inter-Continental Hotels Group and Its Environmental Awareness Programme. In Leslie, D. (ed), *Promoting Environmental Awareness and Action in Hospitality, Tourism and Leisure*. Environment Papers Series No.1, pp. 31-46.

Brandon, P. [2000], cited in SLCCT, Sustainable Development in South Lakeland: Where are we at the start of a new millennium? *Report on the First Annual Event.* South Lakeland Communities Charitable Trust, Kendal. March.

Butler, R. [1993] in Butler, R., and Pearce, D. (eds), *Change in Tourism: People, Places and Processes.* London:Routledge, pp. 1-11.

CC [1993], *Sustainability and the English Countryside–Position Statement.* Countryside Commission, CCP 432. Cheltenham, December.

CEBIS [1996], Tourism: What Does 'Green' Mean? *Sustainability.* Centre for the Environment and Business in Scotland, Scottish Education Forum, Issue 9.

Collier, C. [2000] Presentation by Chief Executive, Cumbria Tourist Board at Fifth Meeting of the Rural Forum for the North West of England. LDNPA, Kendal.

CA [2000] *Tomorrow's Countryside–2020 vision.* Countryside Agency.

ETC/CA [2000], *Rural Tourism: Working for the Countyside: A Consultation Paper by the English Tourism Council and The Countryside Agency.* March, English Tourism Council, London.

Cole, P. [1999] *'Tourism-Wales' Most Sustainable Industry?'*, Paper by Managing Director of Tourism South and West Wales, 19 January.

DCMS [1999], *Tomorrow's Tourism: A Growth Industry for the New Millennium.* Department of Culture, Media and Sport.

DETR [2000a], *Indicators of Sustainable Development.* UK Round Table on Sustainable Development, Department of the Environment, Transport and the Regions, London.

DETR [2000f] *Consultation Paper on Recovery and Recycling Targewts for Packaging Waste in 2001.* Department of the Environment, Transport and the Regions, London. August.

DoE [1996], *Indicators of Sustainable Development for the United Kingdom.* March, Department of the Environment, London: HMSO.

ETB & EDG [1991], *Tourism and the Environment: Maintaining the Balance.* English Tourist Board and the Employment Department Group.

Forte, J.[2000], *Energy: An Issue We Can No Longer Ignore.* Hospitality, February, pp.18-19.

Goodall [1994], Environmental Auditing: Current Best Practice (with Special Reference to British Tourism Firms). in Seaton, A. (ed), *Tourism: The State of the Art.* Wiley and sons, pp. 655-674

Hawkins, R. [1995], The Green Globe Programme: Developing a Greener Future for Travel and Tourism. *Journal of Sustainable Tourism*, Vol 3 (1).

Joy, S. (ed.) [2000], Sheep's Wool-Insulation in Action. *Habitat*, Vol 36 (6), June, The Environment Council. p. 3.

LCC [1999] *Planning, Industrial Development and Tourism Committee.* 10 November.

LDNPA [1997] *The National Park in Figures.* Education Service. Lake District National Park Authority, Cumbria.

LDNPA [1998] *About the National Park.* Education Service. Lake District National Park Authority, Cumbria.

Leslie, D. [1998] *Putting Local Agenda 21 into Practice.* Presentation to National Seminar of the Tourism Management Institute, Leeds. October.

Leslie, D [2001] *An Environmental Audit of the Tourism Industry in the Lake District National Park*. A Report for Friends of the Lake District and the Council for the Protection of Rural England, February.

NFDC [1997], *Our Future Together: A Tourism and Visitor Management Strategy for the New Forest District*. New Forest District Council, Lyndhurst, Hampsire.

Osborn, D. [2000], *Economic Instruments 'Not Too Difficult!'* UK Round Table on Sustainable Development, DETR April, (press release)

PRC (Jersey) [1998] *Jersey in the New Millennium: A Sustainable Future*. Policy and Resources Committee, St Helier, Jersey.

RDC, CC, ETB, WTB, CCW. [1989] *Tourism in national Parks: A Guide to Good Practice*. Rural Development Commission.

RDC, ETB, CC [1991], *The Green Light: A Guide to Sustainable Tourism*. Rural Development Commission, English Tourist Board, Countryside Commission.

RDC [1996], *Green Audit Kit: The DIY Guide to Greening Your Business*. Rural Development Commission.

Wallis, J. and Woodward, S, [1997], Improving the Environmental Performance of Scotland's Hospitality Sector. *International Journal of Hospitality Management*, April, Vol 2 (2), pp. 94-109.

Welford, R. and Starkey, R. [eds] [1996], *The Earthscan Reader in Business and the Environment*. London: Earthscan Publications Ltd.

WTO [1996], *What Tourism Managers Need to Know: a Practical Guide to the Development and Use of Indicators of Sustainable Tourism*. World Tourism Organisation, Madrid.

WTTC, WTO and Earth Council Report [1996], *Agenda 21 For the Travel and Tourism Industry: Towards environmentally Sustainable Development*. World Travel and Tourism Council, Madrid.

Environmental Management Systems for Caribbean Hotels and Resorts: A Case Study of Five Properties in Jamaica

Bill Meade
Joe Pringle

SUMMARY. Hotels and resorts around the world are now adopting environmental management systems as a means of improving resource use efficiency, reducing operating costs, increasing staff involvement and guest awareness, and obtaining international recognition in the travel and tourism marketplace. This article examines the cost savings and performance improvements at five hotel properties in Jamaica that were among the first in the Caribbean to adopt an environmental management system (EMS). The five hotels evaluated in the case study, Sandals Negril, Couples Ocho Rios, Negril Cabins, Swept Away, and Sea Splash have achieved remarkable improvements in environmental performance, and accompanying cost savings, since implementing environmental management systems (EMS).[1] These results are outlined below and serve as direct evidence of environmental performance improvements that result from proactive environmental management.[2] Total cost savings for the five properties is estimated to be $615,500, or $910 per room. The properties had a cumulative water savings of 41.4 million Imperial Gallons (IG) achieved; total electricity savings of 1.67 million kWh; total diesel savings of 169,000 liters; and total Liquefied Petroleum Gas

Bill Meade and Joe Pringle are affiliated with the PA Consulting Group, USA.

[Haworth co-indexing entry note]: "Environmental Management Systems for Caribbean Hotels and Resorts: A Case Study of Five Properties in Jamaica." Meade, Bill, and Joe Pringle. Co-published simultaneously in *Journal of Quality Assurance in Hospitality & Tourism* (The Haworth Hospitality Press, an imprint of The Haworth Press, Inc.) Vol. 2, No. 3/4, 2001, pp. 149-159; and: *Benchmarks in Hospitality and Tourism* (ed: Sungsoo Pyo) The Haworth Hospitality Press, an imprint of The Haworth Press, Inc., 2001, pp. 149-159. Single or multiple copies of this article are available for a fee from The Haworth Document Delivery Service [1-800-HAWORTH, 9:00 a.m. - 5:00 p.m. (EST). E-mail address: getinfo@haworthpressinc.com].

(LPG) savings of 259,000 liters. Expressing overall energy use in terms of kWh,[3] the total energy savings is 5.67 million kWh.

KEYWORDS. Environmental management system, EMS, green hotels, sustainable tourism, operating efficiency, water, energy, solid waste, Jamaica, Caribbean, green globe

BACKGROUND

Environmental management in the hotel industry traces it roots to two major initiatives in the 1990s–Agenda 21 for the Travel and Tourism Industry and ISO 14001. Following the Rio Earth Summit in 1992, the World Tourism Organization and the World Travel and Tourism Council published Agenda 21 for the Travel and Tourism: Toward Environmentally Sustainable Development. Agenda 21 defines a broad array of environmental and social impacts associated with hotel operations and the principles for minimizing these impacts. ISO 14001 is the international environmental management system standard promulgated in 1996 by the Geneva-based International Standards Organization. In 1997, the World Travel and Tourism Council's Green Globe created an international standard and certification program for hotels and other travel and tourism companies that combines the Agenda 21 principles and the ISO 14001 environmental management system–Green Globe 21.

Green Globe is a worldwide certification program dedicated exclusively to helping the travel and tourism industry to develop in a sustainable way. The certification is open to companies and communities of any size, type, or location, and is based on an ISO style of certification. The Green Globe Environmental Management System is similar to that of ISO 14001 and EMAS. It requires an environmental policy, environmental targets and a system to measure performance against those targets, commitment to comply with legal requirements, and communication and documentation procedures. Under the Green Globe 21 standard, facilities must re-certify annually as opposed to every three years with ISO 14001.

There are a number of other international environmental initiatives and eco-labels for the hotel industry. While a discussion of these is beyond the scope of this article, it is important to note that there are many sources of information on best practices for the hotel industry. The distinction of EMS certification schemes such as Green Globe 21 is that they verify that the property has assessed its impacts and designed and implemented a program to minimize those impacts.

An Environmental Management System (EMS) is a systematic framework for integrating environmental management into an organization's activities, products, and services. A critical step in any organization's adoption of an EMS is the identifying those aspects of operations (e.g., use of chemicals in landscaping) and introducing changes in facilities and practices that minimize the impact of the organization on the natural and social environment. The EMS standard distinguishes itself from environmental performance standards in that it focuses on the organizational aspects and the process for determining appropriate levels of environmental performance, rather than prescribing specific technology criteria.

Two concepts that are important in understanding how an EMS works are: (1) continuous improvement and (2) best environmental management practices or "best practices." The concept of continuous improvement implies that the organization can begin at any level of environmental performance. Through an iterative cycle of setting policies, planning environmental objectives and targets, implementing specific actions, measuring the results, and reviewing the overall effectiveness of the program, the organization will optimize its environmental performance over time (see Exhibit 1).

Best practices represent the preferred actions, from an environmental perspective, to perform a given function or service. Because of the similar nature of hotel and resort operations, international organizations have published guidebooks assisting hotel owners and managers determine the appropriate equipment, supplies and changes in staff activities that constitute "best practices".[4] It is important to note that the combination of best practices will differ for properties of different size (small versus large), location (city versus beach), type (business versus leisure) and management (international chain verses independently owned and operated).

EXHIBIT 1. Environmental Management System

SUSTAINABLE TOURISM IN THE CARIBBEAN

The Caribbean remains the world's most tourism-dependent region, with the sector accounting for a quarter of all export earnings, 31% of Gross Domestic Product (GDP) and nearly a half million jobs.[5] Energy and water costs tend to be higher than in the U.S. and other OECD countries. Exhibit 2 illustrates comparative water and electricity costs for selected Caribbean countries. Solid waste management is becoming an increasing issue due to the closure of dumpsites in favor of sanitary landfills and attempts to increase reuse and recycling. Finally, as most of the tourism development is located within sensitive coastal ecosystems, it is no surprise that the Caribbean is also the first region to embrace the concept of sustainable tourism and actively promote environmental management within the hotel industry.

In 1997, the Caribbean Hotel Association formed the Caribbean Alliance for Sustainable Tourism (CAST) to undertake collaborative environmental activities in the hotel and tourism sector, to promote effective management of natural resources, to provide access to expertise on sustainable tourism, and to assist hotel and tourism operations in the Caribbean region to achieve the goals of Agenda 21 for Sustainable Tourism. CAST's Governing Council includes IHEI and Green Globe, as well as a number of prominent hoteliers and active environmental organizations in the region. CAST is also the regional partner for Green Globe 21 EMS Certification.

Also during 1997, the U.S. Agency for International Development launched a new partnership with the Jamaica Hotel and Tourism Association to fund the introduction of environmental management and practices in small hotels (less than 100 rooms). Over three-quarters of all hotel properties in Jamaica, as elsewhere in the Caribbean, are small, locally-owned and operated properties. PA Consulting Group was hired to implement the Environmental Audits for Sustainable Tourism (EAST) program a model for both large hotels in Jamaica, as well as hotels elsewhere in the region.

EXHIBIT 2. Comparative Cost of Water and Electricity

Country	Water Prices ($/m^3)	Electricity Prices ($/kWh)
Barbados	2.1	0.15
Jamaica	2.0	0.13
St. Lucia	2.9	0.21
United States average	.36	0.08
OECD average	.86	0.11

The EAST program began with a demonstration of audits and EMS in small hotels in Negril, and later in Port Antonio. The program included training in auditing for consultants and EMS for hotel managers. It initiated environmental achievement awards for hotels, and an international exchange program[6] to promote environmental leadership and voluntary compliance with environmental standards. The program, now in its fourth year, has become a model for programs in other Caribbean islands.

CASE STUDY OF FIVE JAMAICAN HOTELS

The five hotels described here were selected from over 35 hotels in Jamaica that had undertaken similar efforts because of their successful results. The five hotels were selected because they had implemented a sufficient number of best practices, had an operational EMS in place, and there was adequate data to evaluate cost savings and changes in environmental performance. Between 1998 and 2000, the properties, ranging from 16-rooms to 250-rooms, underwent an intensive program to improve their environmental performance. The two smallest properties are independently owned and operated, while the largest three are part of Jamaican-owned, multi-property groups. Exhibit 3 provides a summary of the five properties. PA assisted two of the properties–Sea Splash and Negril Cabins–under the EAST project. The owners of the other three properties contracted with PA directly for their EMS services.

All five properties underwent the same assistance program and implemented a similar EMS. The assistance program consisted of five steps: (1) assessment, (2) EMS design and documentation, (3) organizational development and training, (4) EMS certification, and (5) performance monitoring. Generally speaking, the programs were implemented over a 1-year period, however, the pace of adoption varied from 9-months to 18-months. In addition to

EXHIBIT 3. Summary of Jamaican Hotels in Case Study

Hotel Name	Location	Number of Rooms
Sea Splash Resort	Negril	15
Negril Cabins Resort	Negril	86
Swept Away Beach Resort and Spa	Negril	134
Couples Ocho Rios	Ocho Rios	172
Sandals Negril Beach Resort and Spa	Negril	223

the on-property efforts and results, the properties have received national and international recognition and have participated in international exchange programs.

Step 1–Assessment. The assessment step involved a detailed diagnostic of current operations and identification of opportunities for improvement. Through an analysis of consumption patterns over a 12-month period preceding the assessment, PA calculated a water and energy use index of consumption per guest night. Baseline water consumption across the five properties varied by a factor of 3.2 times (from 142 IG/GN to 459 IG/GN), while electricity consumption varied by a factor of 2.6 times (from 15.6 kWh/GN to 41.8 kWh/GN). The assessments focused on no-cost or low-cost recommendations that typically pay back in less than 1 year.

Step 2–EMS Design and Documentation. This was perhaps the most difficult step in the process. It required the property management to establish objectives, set targets, assign responsibilities, and document all related activities. The larger properties had a benefit of experience in budgeting capital expenditures and documented standard operating procedures for different departments. It should be noted that while all five properties began with similar EMS Users Manual, each adapted it to fit their needs and other management systems. Maintaining documentation is a requirement of all EMS standards.

Step 3–Organizational Development and Staff Training. Each of the properties appointed an Environmental Officer to lead the property's efforts, and an environmental committee or Green Team. The Environmental Officers were drawn from a wide variety of departments: Accountant (Sea Splash), Property Manager (Negril Cabins), Director of Administration (Swept Away), Executive Housekeeper (Couples Ocho Rios) and Resident Manager (Sandals Negril). Sandals Negril later hired a dedicated Environmental Management Officer. The responsibility of Environmental Officer is an additional duty for the persons in the other four properties. The Green Teams were similarly composed of representatives from engineering, grounds keeping, housekeeping, accounting and the front office. The larger resort properties included a representative of water sports.

Each of the properties went through a similar program of classroom training for management and on-the-job training for line staff. All five properties now include information on their environmental activities in staff orientation. Housekeeping was uniformly the most difficult area to introduce best practices (e.g., towel and linen reuse program) because of high turnover and the routine nature of the work, whereas engineering was the easiest given their familiarity with equipment and hotel operations and utility consumption targets.

Step 4–EMS Certification. Green Globe 21 was selected as the EMS certification because of its direct application to the travel and tourism industry and the support from a regional organization (i.e., CAST) to those interested in pursuing certification. For all five properties, it was the Green Globe 21 certification that motivated the management to fulfill all of the requirements of an EMS, especially the documentation. All five properties achieved Green Globe 21 certification, and several have gone through their first annual re-certification. The shortest length of time from assessment to certification was 9 months (Sandals Negril). The others all took 12-18 months.

Step 5–Monitoring. The old adage–"you can't monitor what you can't measure" holds true here. Each property developed a monitoring program that evaluated the implementation of their EMS (actions achieved versus planned) and the results in their baseline consumption indexes. Each property prepared a monthly report to senior management that summarizes the EMS program. The properties are now able to compare their "pre" and "post" EMS consumption indexes for both water and electricity. Some have extended their monitoring programs to disposable items (e.g., garbage bags and chemical use).

PERFORMANCE IMPROVEMENTS

All five properties experienced an improvement in their water and electricity consumption. The greatest improvement in water use was Swept Away (50% reduction), while the greatest percent improvement in electricity use was Sea Splash (24% reduction). Exhibits 3 and 4 illustrate the "pre" and "post" EMS consumption indexes for water and electricity, respectively.

A summary of the results for the five properties is provided below. It should be noted that these savings have accrued over a 2+ year period, and that while the savings are expected to continue, the year to year improvement is likely to

EXHIBIT 4. Change in Water Consumption

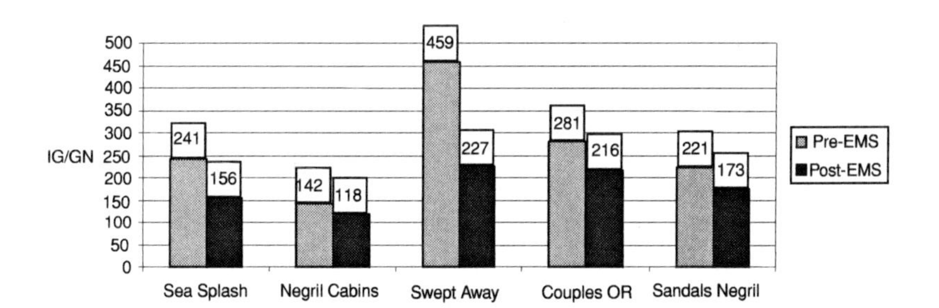

EXHIBIT 5. Change in Electricity Consumption

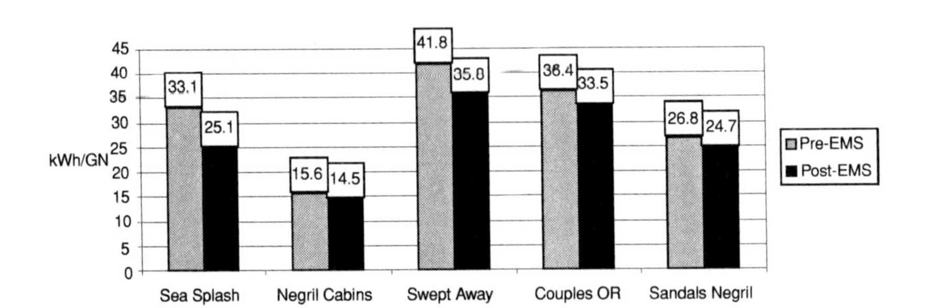

decline as the easiest and most economically attractive "best practices" are adopted.

Sandals Negril (215-rooms) saved approximately 45,000 m^3 of water, 444,000 kilowatt hours of electricity, and 100,000 liters of diesel. In addition, the hotel has achieved a significant reduction in its solid waste stream and realized significant savings of plastic bags and fertilizer. The total investment for the program was approximately $68,000. Based on the estimated savings of $261,000, the program yielded an annual return on investment (ROI) of 190% over the first 2 years. The payback period for the initial investment was approximately 10 months.

Couples Ocho Rios (172-rooms) saved approximately 31,000 m^3 of water and 174,000 kilowatt hours of electricity. The total investment for the program was $50,000: approximately $20,000 in equipment and $30,000 in consulting fees. Based on the estimated savings of $134,000, the program yielded an annual ROI of 200% over the first 16 months. This represents a payback period of just 6 months.

Swept Away (134-rooms) saved approximately 95,000 m^3 of water, 436,000 kilowatt-hours of electricity, 172,000 liters of liquefied petroleum gas and 325,000 liters of diesel. Based on available data, the total investment for the program was approximately $44,000. Based on the estimated savings of $294,000, the program yielded an ROI of 675% over the first 19 months. The payback period for the initial investment was approximately 4 months.

Negril Cabins (80-rooms) saved approximately 11,400 m^3 of water and 145,000 kilowatt hours of electricity. In addition, the hotel has achieved savings of over $5,000 on laundry chemicals since August 1998 through its towel and linen reuse programs and efforts to reduce the use of laundry chemicals. The property began composting in October 1998 and has composted over 35 tons of solid waste. By using this compost for its landscaping needs, the property no longer purchases fertilizer. Based on available data, the total investment in the program was $34,670, and the resulting savings over 2.75 years are estimated to be $46,000, producing an annual ROI of 48%.

Sea Splash (15-rooms) has saved approximately 7,600 m^3 of water and 154,000 kilowatt hours of electricity, leading to significant savings in utility costs. The cost of the project at this resort was $12,259, and the savings since July 1998 are estimated at $46,000, yielding an annual ROI of 151% over the first 2.5 years of the project.

LESSONS LEARNED

The main lesson learned from this case study is that a structured process and management system can yield significant improvements in any size hotel property. As expected, the properties tended to focus on fixing leaks, changes in staff practices (e.g., towel and linen reuse programs) and water conserving devises that pay back in a matter on days or months. Higher cost measures (e.g., high efficiency lighting or water saving toilets) tended to be put off until the second year of EMS implementation when some savings were already realized. In addition to the efficiency improvements, the daily monitoring water and electricity meters saved several of the hotels from erroneous utility bills that would previously have been paid directly from accounting.

Another lesson learned is that an EMS program with reinforcing elements will motivate properties to both enter the program as well as stay in the program. The EMS design without a detailed property assessment makes it difficult for the property to establish realistic targets for improvement and to determine the applicability of "best practices." Similarly, organizational aspects and training are more meaningful when drawn from an EMS that documents job responsibilities, training program, and monitoring program. Certification, by itself, was not viewed as cost-effective without the associated financial savings associated with the assessment recommendations. And finally, measuring the actual results or improvements would not have been possible unless a baseline was established prior to the adoption of an EMS.

A final lesson is that people make the difference. All five properties benefited from strong, and active, support from the General Manager. In the two smaller properties, the owners became more involved in the second year of the programs, and each property's EMS survived changes in General Manager. The two new General Managers have embraced the EMS approach and have further empowered the Environmental Officer and Green Team to lead the property's efforts. Each property has a dynamic individual as their Environmental Officer. These individuals became the "environmental champion" for their properties and were, in four of the five cases, required to take on additional responsibilities. Given that the Environmental Officers are from different departments, it indicates that the character of the individual is as important as their technical knowledge or rank in the hotel. All five properties have found ways to recognize and reward staff for their involvement in their environmental programs. Finally, several of the line staff indicated that they had begun some of the same practices in their homes.

IMPLICATIONS FOR TRANSFERRING RESULTS TO OTHER CARIBBEAN HOTELS AND RESORTS

Transfer of the "Jamaica experience" is well underway. Other Jamaican hotels, including entire hotel groups, have made the commitment to adopt an EMS. USAID has extended its program to additional small hotels in Jamaica, and small hotels in the Eastern Caribbean. Governments of several countries (Bahamas and Cayman Islands) have drawn up plans to sponsor their own EMS demonstration programs. For all intents and purposes, EMS has become a part of the Caribbean hoteliers permanent vocabulary.

As the number of Caribbean hotels with a certified EMS increases, new technical support is emerging. For example, several of the hotels profiled in this case study have already reached out to the hotels operating in their area to provide guidance in adopting "best practices". Hotel training schools are now looking to "green" their curricula by integrating "best practices" into management and line staff training. A training course for "certified" environmental officers is scheduled, and an internship program with hotels in North America is being planned. There is a preliminary plan to establish a Green Hotel Fund that will extend financing for hotels to implement "best practices".

As today's best practices become "common practices" in the Caribbean, the role of organizations like CAST become even more important in researching and analyzing new technologies, products and staff practices to feed the continuous improvement cycle. Combining the competitive nature of the industry that recognizes leaders, and the cooperative spirit of hoteliers helping each other solve common problems in same tourism destination make for powerful forces in optimizing the environmental performance of Caribbean hotels.

NOTES

1. An environmental management system (EMS) is a systematic framework for increasing operating efficiency and improving environmental performance.
2. These results reflect only those that were quantifiable given existing data.
3. The energy content of LPG and diesel is as follows: 1 liter of LPG = 7.09 kWh, and 1 liter of diesel = 10.83 kWh.

4. Environmental Management for Hotels–Industry Guide to Best Practice, prepared by the International Hotel Environment Initiative, 1993.

5. *1999 Caribbean/Latin American Profile,* Caribbean Publishing Company and the Caribbean/Latin American Action. 1998.

6. The Jamaica Hotel and Tourism Association and Fairmont Hotels (formerly Canadian Pacific Hotels) each host as an exchange of environmental officers and members of staff involved in environmental programs.

Index

